CHILDREN'S
ENCYCLOPEDIA
OF PREHISTORIC
LIFE

Dougal Dixon

ARCTURUS

Picture Credits:
Every attempt has been made to clear copyright. Should there be any inadvertent omission,
please apply to the publisher for rectification.

All main illustrations were created by Mat Edwards unless stated below.

Alamy: 14–15 (Stocktrek Images, Inc. / Alamy Stock Photo); **Shutterstock**: 112–113 (aleks1949); 6–7, 20–21, 36–37, 48–49, 56–57, 92–93 (Catmando); 22–23, 24–25, 28–29, 46–47, 60–61, 72–73, 86–87, 88–89, 94–95, 98–99, 102–103, 106–107, 110–111, 120–121, 124–125 (Daniel Eskridge); 34–35, 40–41, 66–67 (Dotted Yeti); 62–63, 90–91 (Elenarts); 18–19, 114–115 (Esteban De Armas); 80–81 (Herschel Hoffmeyer); 82–83 (rodos studio); 52–53 (rodos studio FERHAT CINAR); 68–69 (warpaint); 76–77 (YuRi Photolife).

All other illustrations from Shutterstock or the Arcturus Image Bank.

ARCTURUS
This edition published in 2024 by Arcturus Publishing Limited
26/27 Bickels Yard, 151–153 Bermondsey Street,
London SE1 3HA

Note for readers: In this book, MYA stands for
million years ago.

Author: Dougal Dixon
Consultant: Anne Rooney
Designer: Lorraine Inglis
Editors: Corinna Keefe and Becca Clunes
Picture research: Lorraine Inglis and Paul Futcher
Design manager: Jessica Holliland
Managing editor: Joe Harris

ISBN: 978-1-3988-3582-5
CH010062US
Supplier 29, Date 1023, PI00004275

Printed in China

CONTENTS

Introduction

Earth has not always looked as it does today. Over the last 4.5 billion years, the shapes of the continents, the climate, and the depth of the oceans have been through constant, but extremely slow, changes. Life appeared on Earth almost as soon as the planet's surface was cool enough to support it and since then it has been continually changing and evolving.

Much of what we know about organisms that lived in the distant past comes from fossils. These are records left in rock by things long dead. Fossils can be body parts, such as bones, teeth, and claws, that have mineralized over millions of years. Or they can be impressions left where a body has pressed against clay, mud, or sand that has hardened.

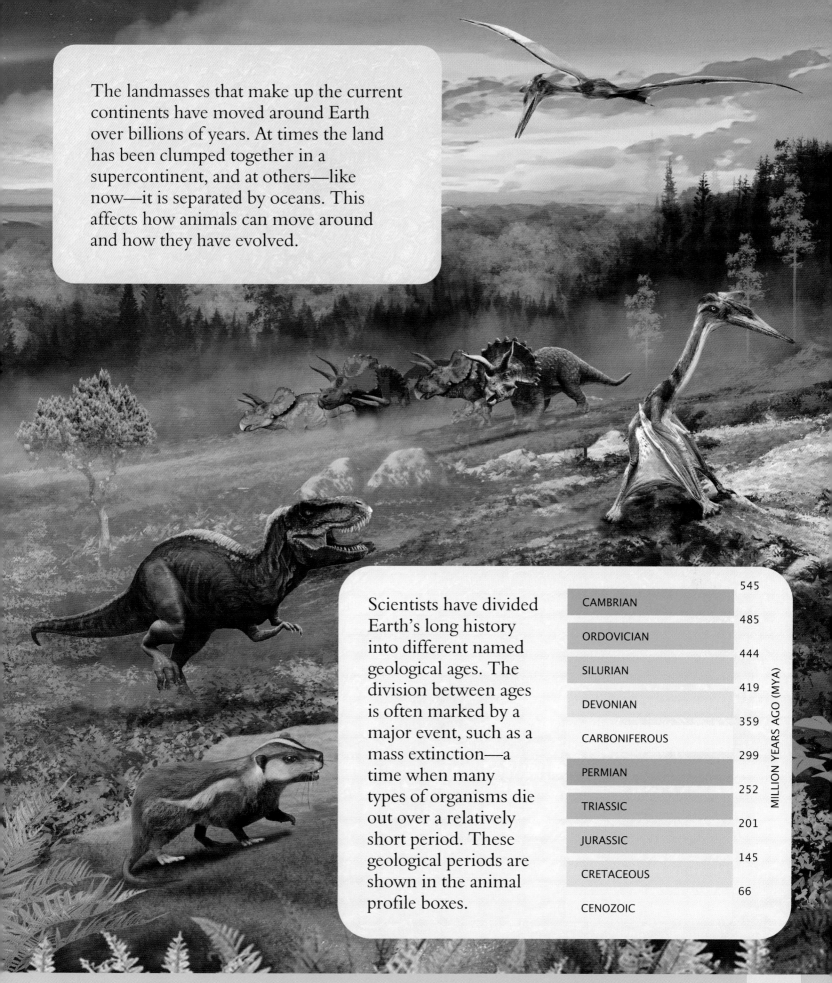

The landmasses that make up the current continents have moved around Earth over billions of years. At times the land has been clumped together in a supercontinent, and at others—like now—it is separated by oceans. This affects how animals can move around and how they have evolved.

Scientists have divided Earth's long history into different named geological ages. The division between ages is often marked by a major event, such as a mass extinction—a time when many types of organisms die out over a relatively short period. These geological periods are shown in the animal profile boxes.

	MILLION YEARS AGO (MYA)
CAMBRIAN	545
ORDOVICIAN	485
SILURIAN	444
DEVONIAN	419
CARBONIFEROUS	359
PERMIAN	299
TRIASSIC	252
JURASSIC	201
CRETACEOUS	145
CENOZOIC	66

DID YOU KNOW? Not many animals get to be fossilized. Fossils are only made in very particular geological conditions. That means we only know about a small proportion of prehistoric creatures.

Chapter 1

Early life

We do not know much about what life was like before 550 million years ago—it is a mystery. That is because all the animals that did exist in those ancient times were soft and boneless. They did not have hard parts that could be preserved. Then everything changed.

Some animals swam in the sea like fish. Others grew like plants, stuck to the seabed, or walked around on the ocean floor.

The First Fossils

Suddenly, at the beginning of what we call the Cambrian period, hard shells and skeletons appeared. All sorts of animals that could grow hard parts lived in the oceans. Some had shells of calcite like snails and clams. Others had coverings of chitin, tough and flexible, like your fingernails. Some, such as sponges, had glasslike frameworks. All of these hard parts were strong enough to be preserved as fossils.

Most Cambrian animals were unlike anything we find today. It was a time of experimentation.

Before the Cambrian, animals were built like soft, water-filled balloons, with no hard parts.

DID YOU KNOW? The best place to find the weird animals of the Cambrian is on a mountainside in British Columbia, Canada.

505 MYA

CAMBRIAN
ORDOVICIAN
SILURIAN
DEVONIAN
CARBONIFEROUS
PERMIAN
TRIASSIC
JURASSIC
CRETACEOUS
CENOZOIC

Name: *Opabinia*
(oh-pa-BIN-ee-ah)
Family: Opabiniidae
Length: 7 cm (3 in)

ANIMAL PROFILE

About the size
of your thumb,
Opabinia was flexible
like a shrimp. It had
a food-snatching
trunk and five
eyes!

Muddy Preservation

In these early times, all complex living things
existed in the oceans. The land was barren
and the atmosphere unbreathable. When
creatures died, some of them sank to the
seabed, were covered in mud or sand,
and preserved as fossils.

Sometimes a fossil is just the
impression left behind by a creature,
not a part of the body itself.

Orthoceras

Most of the strange, experimental animals of the Cambrian period died out, but some became the ancestors of all the animals after them. One successful group were what we call the cephalopods—the "head-footed" animals. These had tentacles growing from their heads.

Head in a Shell

Modern cephalopods—like octopus and squid—do not have shells, but the ancient ones did. Often the shell was coiled like a snail, but sometimes it was straight and conical. *Orthoceras* was a cephalopod with a conical shell. The tentacles surrounding its mouth were used to catch food and pull it in.

A fossil *Orthoceras* shows how the shell is divided into chambers.

An octopus has suckers on its tentacles. These have tiny hard hooks to help to grab prey. Sometimes we find these hooks as fossils.

A Long-Term Survivor

The modern octopus is the most familiar of the surviving cephalopods. It has no shell. There were shell-less octopuses in ancient times as well, but we do not find their remains often. With no shell, they do not become fossils easily.

Orthoceras lived in the front of its shell, while the shell chambers behind it were full of air. By adjusting the amount of trapped air, *Orthoceras* could float at different levels.

Orthoceras could move swiftly backward like a rocket, by blasting water through a tube among its tentacles.

A cephalopod tentacle is nearly all muscle. There are no bones or shelly parts.

460 MYA

CAMBRIAN | ORDOVICIAN | SILURIAN | DEVONIAN | CARBONIFEROUS | PERMIAN | TRIASSIC | JURASSIC | CRETACEOUS | CENOZOIC

Name: *Orthoceras* (OR–tho–SER–as)
Class: Cephalopoda
Length: 4.5 m (14 ft), but usually smaller

ANIMAL PROFILE

DID YOU KNOW? The straight-shelled cephalopods existed for about 200 million years, from Ordovician to Permian times.

Dunkleosteus

During the Cambrian period, some animals began to evolve a flexible, jointed skeleton inside their bodies. These creatures looked a bit like worms. Later, fish would evolve from them, too. Eventually, amphibians and reptiles would evolve from fish to become the biggest of the land-living animals.

The Fish Take Over

The fish were the earliest of the vertebrates—the animals with a backbone—and became established in the Devonian period. One of the earliest groups of fish were the arthrodires. *Dunkleosteus* was one of the biggest and fiercest of these. It had a streamlined, torpedo-like body, and its front was protected by bony plates. It had no teeth, but the plates around its mouth made sharp-edged cutting weapons.

The fish not only ruled the oceans, but thrived in freshwater rivers and lakes as well.

We only know of the head and neck shield of *Dunkleosteus*. We are not really sure what the rest of the body was like.

Jawless Ancestors

The earliest fish—before *Dunkleosteus* and the rest of the arthrodires appeared—were a group of fish that had no jaws. Their mouths were mere suckers. They used them to suck up smaller creatures from the seafloor for food. Jaws and teeth did not evolve until later.

Pteraspis was a jawless fish from the Devonian period. It fed by sucking in floating plankton as it swam.

DID YOU KNOW? You and I still possess fish scales—our teeth! Yes, our teeth are actually highly modified fish scales.

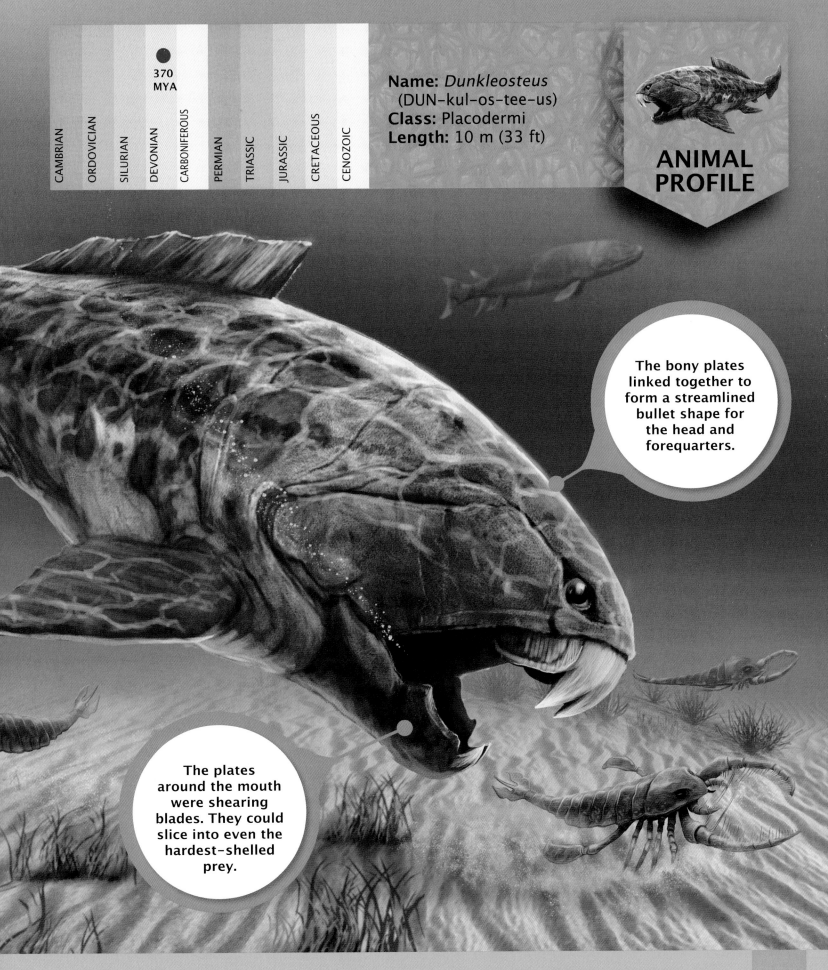

CAMBRIAN ORDOVICIAN SILURIAN DEVONIAN CARBONIFEROUS PERMIAN TRIASSIC JURASSIC CRETACEOUS CENOZOIC

370 MYA

Name: *Dunkleosteus*
(DUN–kul–os–tee–us)
Class: Placodermi
Length: 10 m (33 ft)

ANIMAL PROFILE

The bony plates linked together to form a streamlined bullet shape for the head and forequarters.

The plates around the mouth were shearing blades. They could slice into even the hardest-shelled prey.

Tiktaalik

The first vertebrates to venture out of the water and onto land were specialized fish. They could breathe air and move on the ground using muscular fins. Later, they would evolve into the first amphibians—but in between came animals that were not quite fish and not quite amphibians.

Two Homes

During the Devonian period, several types of fish began to develop features that would help them live on dry land. *Tiktaalik* was one of these. It was a fish, with fins and gills. But its fins were strong enough to carry its weight on land, and its gills were helped by lungs that could breathe air. With its flat head and the lack of a dorsal fin on its back, it looked more like a crocodile than a fish.

Tiktaalik had a neck—something not seen in fish. This would have helped it hunt on land.

The bones of the skull suggest that *Tiktaalik* breathed air through lungs more easily than it absorbed oxygen through gills.

By Devonian times, land plants had evolved which converted Earth's toxic atmosphere into breathable oxygen.

DID YOU KNOW? The ability to live on land probably came about when water–living animals lost their homes to droughts and needed to move to new ponds.

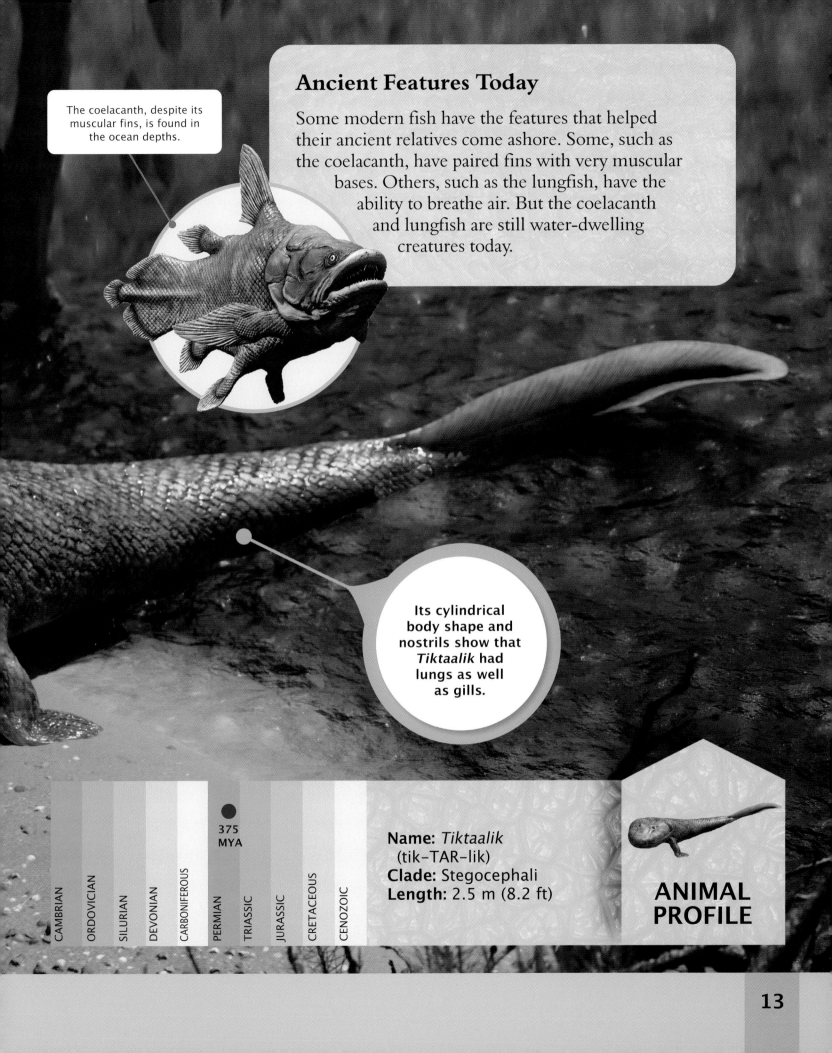

Ancient Features Today

Some modern fish have the features that helped their ancient relatives come ashore. Some, such as the coelacanth, have paired fins with very muscular bases. Others, such as the lungfish, have the ability to breathe air. But the coelacanth and lungfish are still water-dwelling creatures today.

The coelacanth, despite its muscular fins, is found in the ocean depths.

Its cylindrical body shape and nostrils show that *Tiktaalik* had lungs as well as gills.

375 MYA

CAMBRIAN

ORDOVICIAN

SILURIAN

DEVONIAN

CARBONIFEROUS

PERMIAN

TRIASSIC

JURASSIC

CRETACEOUS

CENOZOIC

Name: *Tiktaalik* (tik–TAR–lik)
Clade: Stegocephali
Length: 2.5 m (8.2 ft)

ANIMAL PROFILE

Diplocaulus

As the Devonian period passed into the Carboniferous and then the Permian, the amphibians got better at living on land. However, they still needed to come back to the water to breed and lay their eggs. They couldn't live in very dry areas.

Different Lifestyles

There were amphibians that spent most of their time in the water, only coming out onto land briefly. There were amphibians that spent nearly all their lives on land, hardly ever getting wet. Some lost all their limbs and lived like eels or snakes. *Diplocaulus* lived in streams and rivers using its boomerang-like head as a hydrofoil (a shape that provides lift in the water), which helped it move about in the current.

Crassygyrinus from the Carboniferous is an example of an amphibian that spent most of its life in water.

253 MYA

CAMBRIAN	ORDOVICIAN	SILURIAN	DEVONIAN	CARBONIFEROUS	PERMIAN	TRIASSIC	JURASSIC	CRETACEOUS	CENOZOIC

Name: *Diplocaulus*
(dip–LOH–cor–lus)
Subclass: Lepospondyli
Length: 1 m (3.3 ft)

ANIMAL PROFILE

The name *Cacops* means "ugly face" because of its strangely oversized skull and heavy shoulders.

Protective Plates

Cacops, from the Permian, is an example of an amphibian that was almost totally adapted to life on land. It had protective plates along its back to defend itself against big, meat-eating reptiles.

Diplocaulus lay on riverbeds with its hydrofoil head facing upstream, catching food as it floated by.

Small legs show that *Diplocaulus* did not spend much time on land.

Diplocaulus lived in North America and Africa. It was the biggest of the lepospondyl amphibian group.

DID YOU KNOW? The head of a young *Diplocaulus* was quite narrow. It only developed the boomerang shape as it aged.

Meganeurites

The first animals to leave the sea and colonize the land in Devonian times were the arthropods—animals with jointed legs, like insects and spiders. By the Carboniferous period, they had grown to huge sizes because the atmosphere was rich in oxygen from plants.

Flying Hunters

Meganeurites was one of the giant dragonflies of Carboniferous times. It was the top flying predator of the skies and hunted other insects. The first giant dragonfly to be discovered was *Meganeura*, but its fossils are very scrappy. Its relative, *Meganeurites*, is much better known.

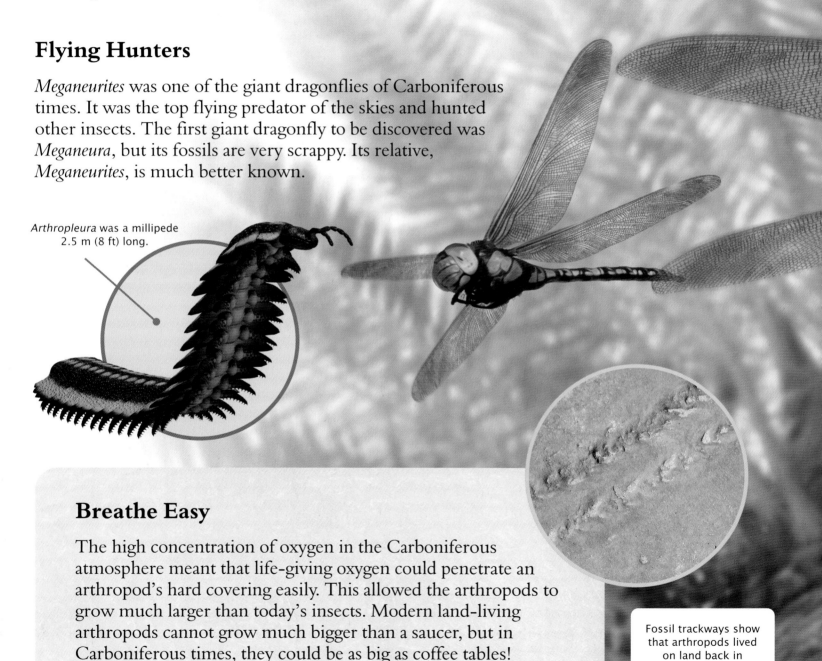

Arthropleura was a millipede 2.5 m (8 ft) long.

Breathe Easy

The high concentration of oxygen in the Carboniferous atmosphere meant that life-giving oxygen could penetrate an arthropod's hard covering easily. This allowed the arthropods to grow much larger than today's insects. Modern land-living arthropods cannot grow much bigger than a saucer, but in Carboniferous times, they could be as big as coffee tables!

Fossil trackways show that arthropods lived on land back in Devonian times.

The wingspan of *Meganeurites* was so big that it probably hunted in open areas, rather than between trees in the forests.

The name *Meganeurites* means "great nerves"— the network of veins that support the long wings.

The legs of *Meganeurites* were covered in barbs to enable the great insect to catch prey on the wing.

300 MYA

CAMBRIAN
ORDOVICIAN
SILURIAN
DEVONIAN
CARBONIFEROUS
PERMIAN
TRIASSIC
JURASSIC
CRETACEOUS
CENOZOIC

Name: *Meganeurites*
(meg–AN–er–ites)
Class: Insecta
Wingspan: 70 cm (28 in)
Weight: 150 g (5.3 oz)

ANIMAL PROFILE

DID YOU KNOW? The compound eyes of *Meganeurites* went all around its head. It could see its prey in all directions.

Scutosaurus

By Permian times, the reptiles were established on land. They did not need to go back to ponds to lay eggs, like amphibians did. Their secret was to lay eggs that were covered in a hard shell and were lined with a waterproof membrane—like a private, shielded pond for each youngster.

Scutosaurus' skull was massive and bony, with spikes sticking out at the side. The spikes were probably forprotection.

Prehistoric Plant-Eaters

Most of the early reptiles were meat-eating, hunting animals. But they soon developed the ability to eat and digest plants. The pareiasaurs were early plant-eating reptiles. Eating plants needs a much bigger digestive system than eating meat, and this meant a bigger body. The pareiasaurs ranged in size from rabbit-sized to as big as a rhinoceros. *Scutosaurus* was one of the biggest pareiasaurs.

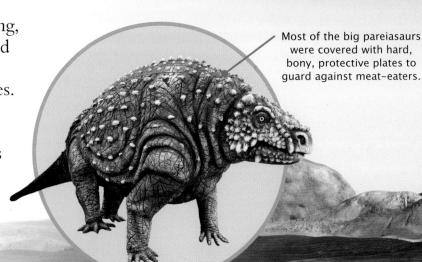

Most of the big pareiasaurs were covered with hard, bony, protective plates to guard against meat-eaters.

Glossopteris was a seed fern that grew like a tree. It was food for early plant–eating animals, like *Scutosaurus*.

Changing Plants

It was not just reptiles that changed and adapted to new conditions. New kinds of plants were appearing as well. There were no flowering plants or grasses yet. The vegetation consisted mostly of ferns and conifers. A common plant was what we call a "seed fern."

Huge hips, shoulders, and limbs were needed to support its great weight.

Scutosaurus lived in a desert area. It probably had to travel long distances between oases to find food.

260 MYA

CAMBRIAN
ORDOVICIAN
SILURIAN
DEVONIAN
CARBONIFEROUS
PERMIAN
TRIASSIC
JURASSIC
CRETACEOUS
CENOZOIC

Name: *Scutosaurus*
(scoot-oh-SORE-us)
Class: Reptilia
Length: 3 m (9ft 10 in)
Weight: 1,160 kg (2,560 lb)

ANIMAL PROFILE

DID YOU KNOW? We think that the pareiasaurs were the ancestors of today's turtles.

Mesosaurus

Some of the first fully land-living animals were reptiles—the animals we know today as lizards, snakes, crocodiles, and turtles. However, many of the fossil reptiles we have found were water-living rather than land-living types. *Mesosaurus* was one of the earliest of these.

Although it was a water-living animal, the joints of *Mesosaurus'* legs show that it could move about on land like a turtle.

Distant Cousins

With its snaky body, its long, finned tail, and its webbed feet, *Mesosaurus* was obviously a swimming reptile. But it lived in shallow or fresh water. So why are its fossils found in South Africa and on the other side of the Atlantic Ocean, in Brazil? The answer is that these two continents were joined together in Permian times, when the Atlantic Ocean did not exist. In fact, all the continents were fused into one single landmass, called Pangea.

It is easier for fossils to form in water than on land. Most fossils of *Mesosaurus* are of youngsters, suggesting that the young spent more time in the water than the adults did.

DID YOU KNOW? Like *Lystrosaurus* (see page 38), the fossils of *Mesosaurus* show that all the continents were joined together in Permian times.

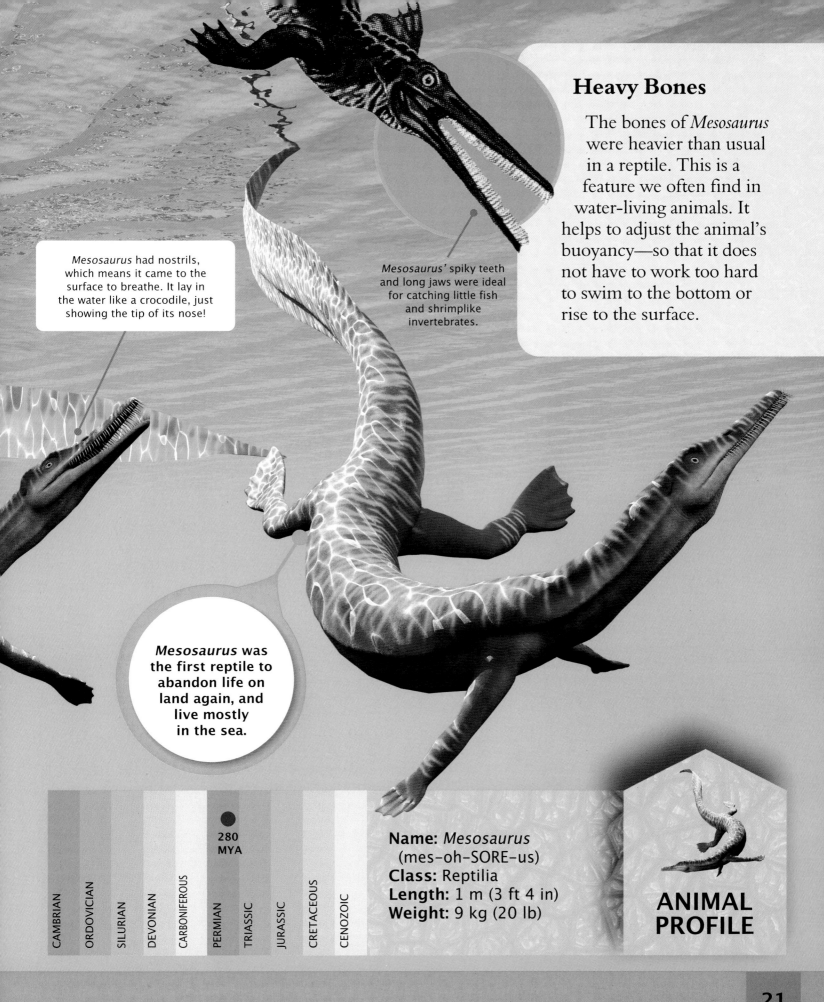

Heavy Bones

The bones of *Mesosaurus* were heavier than usual in a reptile. This is a feature we often find in water-living animals. It helps to adjust the animal's buoyancy—so that it does not have to work too hard to swim to the bottom or rise to the surface.

Mesosaurus had nostrils, which means it came to the surface to breathe. It lay in the water like a crocodile, just showing the tip of its nose!

Mesosaurus' spiky teeth and long jaws were ideal for catching little fish and shrimplike invertebrates.

Mesosaurus was the first reptile to abandon life on land again, and live mostly in the sea.

280 MYA

CAMBRIAN | ORDOVICIAN | SILURIAN | DEVONIAN | CARBONIFEROUS | PERMIAN | TRIASSIC | JURASSIC | CRETACEOUS | CENOZOIC

Name: *Mesosaurus* (mes-oh-SORE-us)
Class: Reptilia
Length: 1 m (3 ft 4 in)
Weight: 9 kg (20 lb)

ANIMAL PROFILE

Dimetrodon

As the reptiles spread through the world in the Permian period, they developed into a number of different lines, all from small, lizard-like animals. One line would eventually become dinosaurs. Another line gave rise to the mammals, including humans. The early forms of this line are called the paramammals, and included the sail-backed *Dimetrodon*.

Radiator-Back

Dimetrodon looked like a huge lizard with an enormous sail on its back. It was an active hunter and preyed on the other big reptiles and amphibians of the early Permian desert plains and streams. The sail may have worked as a heat-exchanger, turning to the sun in the early morning to catch the warmth, then turning into the wind to cool off later in the day.

The sail was covered in skin. It was probably brightly–patterned and used as a signal.

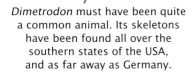

Dimetrodon must have been quite a common animal. Its skeletons have been found all over the southern states of the USA, and as far away as Germany.

The name "*Dimetrodon*" means "two shapes of teeth." It had long teeth for killing at the front of the mouth, and smaller teeth at the back.

DID YOU KNOW? We often see *Dimetrodon* called a dinosaur, but it actually was not. It lived 50 million years before the dinosaurs appeared.

CAMBRIAN	ORDOVICIAN	SILURIAN	DEVONIAN	CARBONIFEROUS	PERMIAN	TRIASSIC	JURASSIC	CRETACEOUS	CENOZOIC

280 MYA

Name: *Dimetrodon*
(dy–MET–roh–don)
Clade: Synapsida
Length: 4.6 m (15 ft)
Weight: 250 kg (550 lb)

ANIMAL PROFILE

The sail was supported by long spines, each one growing from a vertebra (small bone) of the back.

Other Sailbacks

Dimetrodon was not the only animal with a sail on its back at that time. Several of its relatives—a group we call the spehenacodonts—had them as well. Some were actually plant-eaters. There was even a sail-backed, land-living amphibian called *Platyhystrix*. They may have developed their sails to keep cool in the hot desert air.

Edaphosaurus was one of the plant–eating sphenacodonts related to *Dimetrodon*.

23

Gorgonops

Towards the end of the Permian period, paramammals became more mammal-like. Some of them adopted lifestyles that would be familiar to us. Small ones hunted like weasels, while big ones hunted like lions. *Gorgonops* was about the size of a wolf, and it would have hunted like a wolf, too.

Main Hunter

If you wondered what caused the pareiasaurs (see page 18) to develop their protective bony shields, then *Gorgonops* was the answer. It preyed on all the other animals of the late Permian deserts. It had long, curved teeth that would have sliced through the thick hides of the biggest plant-eating animals around.

Like the mammals to come, *Gorgonops* was probably warm-blooded. That meant it could stay active longer, but it also needed more food than a cold-blooded animal.

Gorgonops may have been covered in fur. If so, the fur may have been patterned like a hunting mammal of today,

260 MYA

CAMBRIAN | ORDOVICIAN | SILURIAN | DEVONIAN | CARBONIFEROUS | PERMIAN | TRIASSIC | JURASSIC | CRETACEOUS | CENOZOIC

Name: *Gorgonops*
(GOR-gon-ops)
Clade: Therapsida
Length: 2 m (6 ft 7 in)
Weight: 300 kg (660 lb)

ANIMAL PROFILE

DID YOU KNOW? The inside of *Gorgonops'* nose was very complicated. It may have used its sense of smell, rather than hearing or sight, for hunting.

A Third Eye

Like many reptiles, but unlike mammals, *Gorgonops* had a gap in the top of its skull that held a light-sensitive organ. It helped *Gorgonops* to maintain its daytime and nighttime body rhythms.

The pineal organ is sometimes called a third "eye."

Its jaws could gape open about 90 degrees, giving the killing teeth a strong slashing action.

Have you seen a crocodile run? *Gorgonops* would have held its legs the same way—not quite straight and not quite upright.

Chapter 2

A new beginning

The Permian period ended with several huge volcanic eruptions. Many plants and creatures died out—but then, in the Triassic period, new plants began to clothe the Earth. Strange new creatures evolved, too, such as *Shringasaurus*. *Shringasaurus* was not a dinosaur, but it was a big plant-eater, adapted to feeding from tall trees.

A New Family

The allokotosaurs were big, lumbering plant-eaters that only existed for a few million years in the middle to late Triassic. *Shringasaurus* was the strangest of these, with its massive neck and its pair of horns. At the end of the Triassic period, the allokotosaurs were replaced by the long-necked plant-eating sauropod dinosaurs.

Shringasaurus had an unusual body shape. Its limbs were partly spread, like a crocodile, not upright like a dinosaur.

Fighting with Horns

Some *Shringasaurus* individuals had horns, and some did not. Perhaps only males had them. They might have used them to fight for the right to lead the herd, as we see in modern horned animals.

Like modern goats, the horns of *Shringasaurus* had bony cores surrounded with keratin (the same material found in your fingernails).

Name: *Shringasaurus*
(shrin-ga-SORE-us)
Clade: Allokotosauria
Height: 2 m (6 ft)
Length: 4 m (13 ft)
Weight: 1,000 kg (2,200 lb)

ANIMAL
PROFILE

245
MYA

CAMBRIAN
ORDOVICIAN
SILURIAN
DEVONIAN
CARBONIFEROUS
PERMIAN
TRIASSIC
JURASSIC
CRETACEOUS
CENOZOIC

Tall *Glossopteris* seed-fern
trees provided food for
Shringasaurus and its relatives.

The small
head was held high,
enabling *Shringasaurus*
to eat from tall trees
where other animals
could not reach.

Shringasaurus had flat
feet, like a bear.

DID YOU KNOW? *Shringasaurus* had teeth all across the roof
of its mouth. They must have acted like a vegetable grater.

Shonisaurus

After the mass extinction at the end of the Permian period, the oceans were almost dead. But after a while, life began to return to them. Some groups of land vertebrates left the land and became sea-living animals again. They developed streamlined shapes, flippers, and fins, just like their fishy ancestors.

Its smooth skin and shark-like back and tail fins enabled huge *Shonisaurus* to slip though the water easily.

Like a Fish

The ichthyosaurs were the most fishlike of the sea-living animals of the Triassic and Jurassic periods. If you saw an ichthyosaur, you would have thought it was a shark or a dolphin. Like them, it had developed features that enabled it to thrive in the water. There were many Triassic ichthyosaurs, ranging from the dolphin-sized *Grippia* to *Shonisaurus*, which was as big as a whale.

Grippia   *Shonisaurus*

230 MYA

CAMBRIAN	ORDOVICIAN	SILURIAN	DEVONIAN	CARBONIFEROUS	PERMIAN	TRIASSIC	JURASSIC	CRETACEOUS	CENOZOIC

Name: *Shonisaurus*
(SHON-ee-SORE-us)
Order: Ichthyosauria
Length: 15 m (49 ft)
Weight: 30 tonnes (33 tons)

ANIMAL PROFILE

DID YOU KNOW? *Shonisaurus* is the state fossil of Nevada, where most fossils have been found.

Breathing Air

Shonisaurus may have had all the appearance of a fish, but it had no gills, so it could not breathe underwater. It had nostrils and lungs instead. Like a whale, it had to come to the surface of the sea to take a breath.

Shonisaurus had long, narrow jaws, good for catching fish.

Sharks were one of the groups of fish that survived the end–Permian extinction. They flourished in Triassic seas.

Its **fingers** were **fused into a paddle** that helped *Shonisaurus* to **steer**.

Megalancosaurus

It took a long time for plant life to spread over the volcano-blasted landscape of the Triassic period. First came an undergrowth of ferns. Soon, there were forests of trees—mostly conifers and tree ferns. All sorts of animals lived in these trees.

Tree Climbers

Insects buzzed about in the branches and leaves, and small tree-living animals evolved to hunt them. *Megalancosaurus* was one of these. Its long limbs and its ability to climb have led some scientists to nickname *Megalancosaurus* and its relatives the "monkey lizards." Some of its close relatives were able to glide, like flying squirrels. Others could burrow in the ground, like moles. The small reptiles of this period could adapt to almost any lifestyle.

Petrified trees in Arizona, USA, are the remains of a Triassic forest in which *Megalancosaurus* lived.

Megalancosaurus had eyes that pointed forward. This helped it to judge the distance to fast-moving insect prey.

DID YOU KNOW? There were at least two species of *Megalancosaurus*. One had toes for clambering along thin twigs. The other preferred to cling to tree trunks.

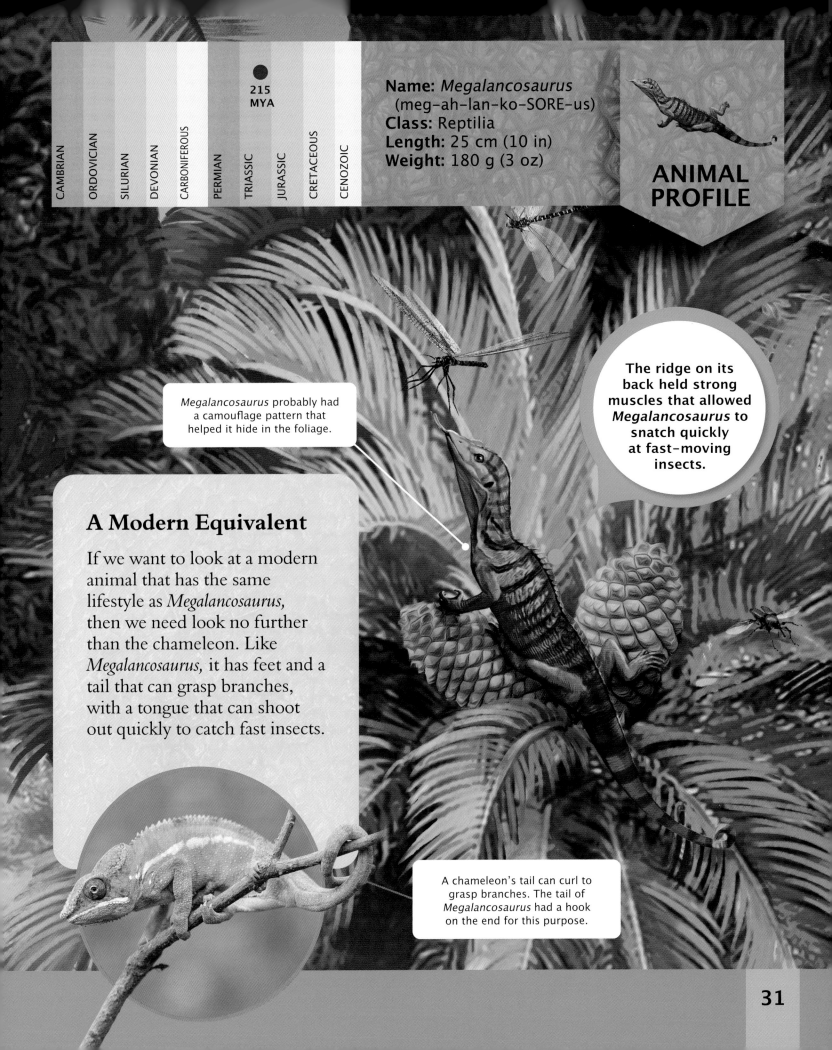

CAMBRIAN	ORDOVICIAN	SILURIAN	DEVONIAN	CARBONIFEROUS	PERMIAN	TRIASSIC	JURASSIC	CRETACEOUS	CENOZOIC

215 MYA

Name: *Megalancosaurus*
(meg-ah-lan-ko-SORE-us)
Class: Reptilia
Length: 25 cm (10 in)
Weight: 180 g (3 oz)

ANIMAL PROFILE

Megalancosaurus probably had a camouflage pattern that helped it hide in the foliage.

The ridge on its back held strong muscles that allowed *Megalancosaurus* to snatch quickly at fast-moving insects.

A Modern Equivalent

If we want to look at a modern animal that has the same lifestyle as *Megalancosaurus,* then we need look no further than the chameleon. Like *Megalancosaurus,* it has feet and a tail that can grasp branches, with a tongue that can shoot out quickly to catch fast insects.

A chameleon's tail can curl to grasp branches. The tail of *Megalancosaurus* had a hook on the end for this purpose.

31

Icarosaurus

Vertebrate life spread everywhere in the Triassic period—mostly on land and in the sea—but it also spread into the skies. Some treetop-living forest animals soon picked up the knack of jumping and gliding from one tree to another. They did not have wings. Instead, they used parachute structures formed from extended rib bones.

The Parachuting Lizard

Icarosaurus was a tiny lizard-like animal that could jump from a branch, spread out its ribs like an umbrella, and fall gently into the branches of a nearby tree. By doing this, it could travel from tree to tree to find more food or even to escape enemies. It was only the size of a large moth, but some of its gliding relatives at that time were as big as parrots.

The parachute skin of *Icarosaurus* would have camouflaged it against a tree trunk when spread out at rest.

In flight, the whole animal would have been flat to slide through the air.

DID YOU KNOW? The only *Icarosaurus* fossil ever found was discovered accidentally by three teenagers.

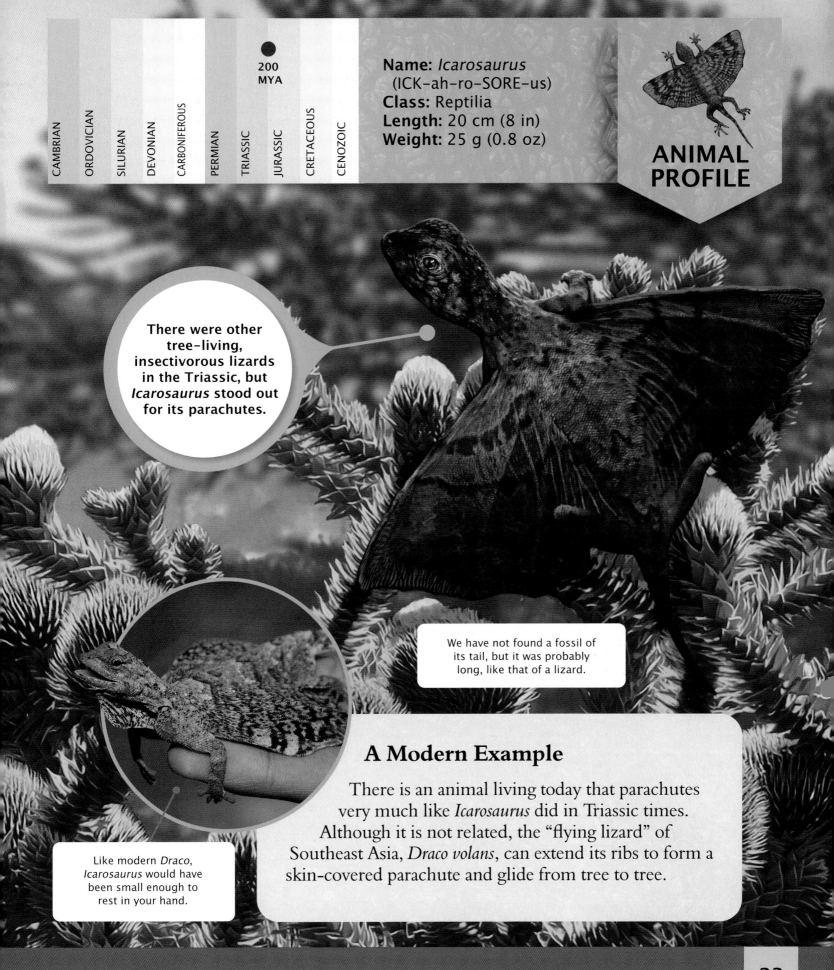

CAMBRIAN
ORDOVICIAN
SILURIAN
DEVONIAN
CARBONIFEROUS
PERMIAN
TRIASSIC
JURASSIC
CRETACEOUS
CENOZOIC

200 MYA

Name: *Icarosaurus*
(ICK–ah–ro–SORE–us)
Class: Reptilia
Length: 20 cm (8 in)
Weight: 25 g (0.8 oz)

ANIMAL PROFILE

There were other tree-living, insectivorous lizards in the Triassic, but *Icarosaurus* stood out for its parachutes.

We have not found a fossil of its tail, but it was probably long, like that of a lizard.

Like modern *Draco*, *Icarosaurus* would have been small enough to rest in your hand.

A Modern Example

There is an animal living today that parachutes very much like *Icarosaurus* did in Triassic times. Although it is not related, the "flying lizard" of Southeast Asia, *Draco volans*, can extend its ribs to form a skin-covered parachute and glide from tree to tree.

Tanystropheus

In Triassic times, a vast ocean named the Tethys separated the continents that would later become Europe and Africa. At its northern edge, shallow seas covered much of modern Europe. The Tethys would become narrower over time as the continents moved toward one another. Along the European coastline were shallow seas and bays, in which lived some of the strangest creatures ever.

What a Long Neck!

Imagine an animal like a big lizard, with sprawling limbs and a long tail. Now imagine it with a neck that was longer than the body and the tail together. You have imagined *Tanystropheus*.

Many fossils of this strange animal have been found in Italy, in rocks laid down in shallow seas. It lived along the shorelines, sometimes on land and sometimes in the water, and hunted fish.

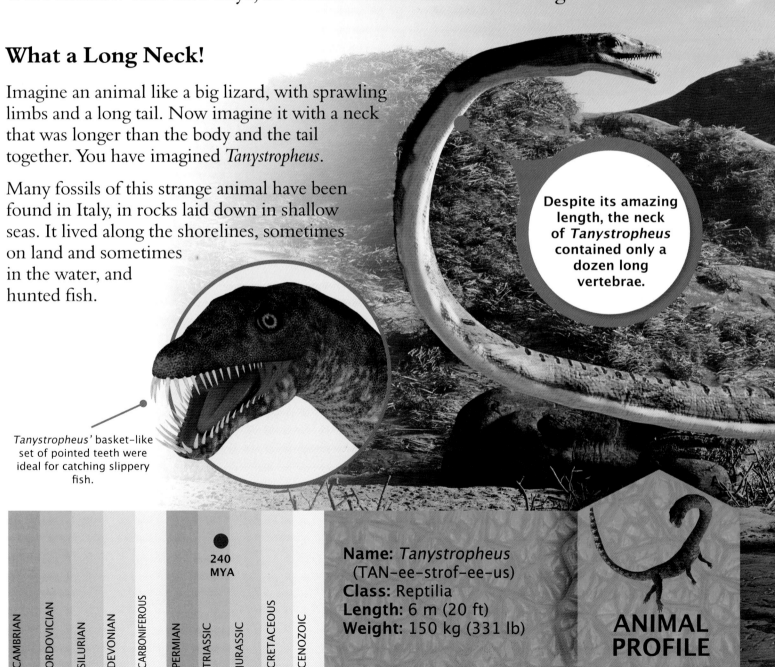

Despite its amazing length, the neck of *Tanystropheus* contained only a dozen long vertebrae.

Tanystropheus' basket–like set of pointed teeth were ideal for catching slippery fish.

240 MYA

CAMBRIAN	ORDOVICIAN	SILURIAN	DEVONIAN	CARBONIFEROUS	PERMIAN	TRIASSIC	JURASSIC	CRETACEOUS	CENOZOIC

Name: *Tanystropheus*
(TAN–ee–strof–ee–us)
Class: Reptilia
Length: 6 m (20 ft)
Weight: 150 kg (331 lb)

ANIMAL PROFILE

Swimming Like a Frog

Tanystropheus had longer hind legs than front legs. From this, we can gather that it swam like a frog—kicking together with its hind legs and not using its front legs at all. Fossil footprints made in shallow water mud suggest that this is how *Tanystropheus* swam in the shallow sea.

While underwater, *Tanystropheus* could snatch at fish with its long neck.

On shore, *Tanystropheus* could have used its neck to reach into the water and catch fish.

The legs and feet show that it was just as happy in the water as on land.

DID YOU KNOW? The neck bones of **Tanystropheus** are so long that the fossils were once thought to have been wing bones from a flying animal.

35

Placodus

The edges of the Tethys ocean in Triassic times teemed with plants and small sea creatures. The shallow waters were alive with seaweeds, corals, and shellfish. Many different kinds of animals developed to exploit all this food.

Shellfish-Eater

A big shellfish-eater of modern times is the walrus. *Placodus* was a reptile that lived a bit like a walrus, but it was shaped more like a giant newt or a large, blubbery lizard. Its big solid body with heavy bones helped to keep its position in the water. It moved about with its legs on land and swam with its flattened tail in the sea.

The back of the mouth had broad, flat teeth for crushing shellfish.

Protruding tusk–like teeth plucked shellfish from the rocks.

Another strange aquatic reptile of the time was *Atopodentatus*, which had broad jaws for grazing seaweed from rocks.

DID YOU KNOW? *Placodus* had a pineal organ (see page 25) on top of its head. This organ was sensitive to light and used for balance and orientation.

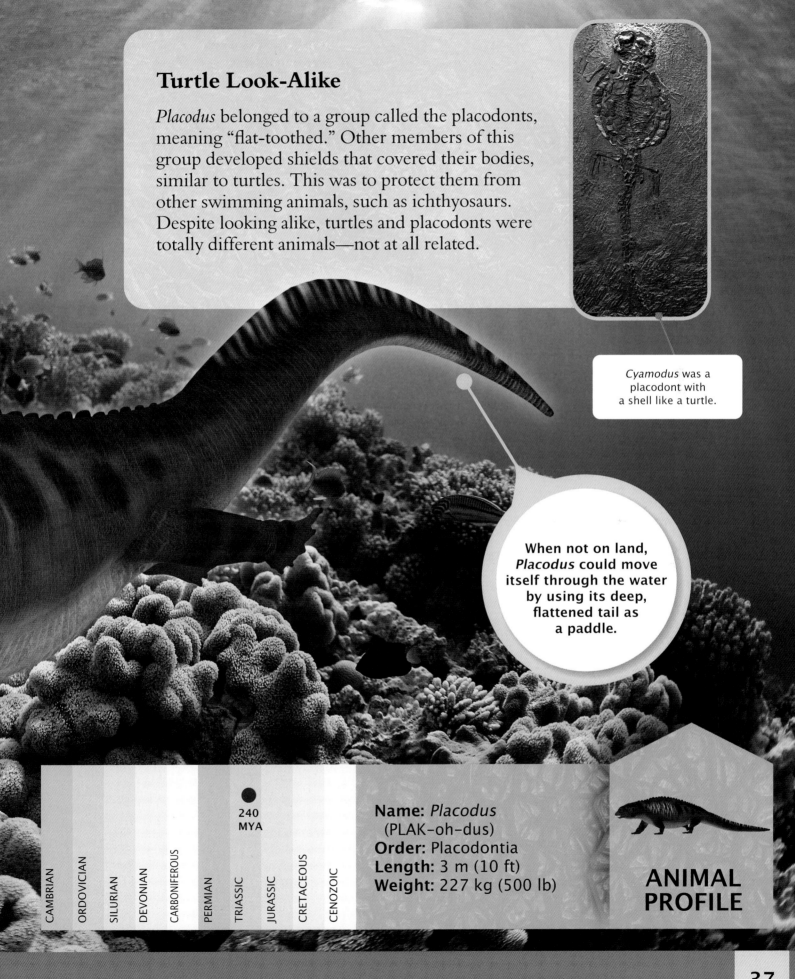

Turtle Look-Alike

Placodus belonged to a group called the placodonts, meaning "flat-toothed." Other members of this group developed shields that covered their bodies, similar to turtles. This was to protect them from other swimming animals, such as ichthyosaurs. Despite looking alike, turtles and placodonts were totally different animals—not at all related.

Cyamodus was a placodont with a shell like a turtle.

When not on land, *Placodus* could move itself through the water by using its deep, flattened tail as a paddle.

240 MYA

CAMBRIAN

ORDOVICIAN

SILURIAN

DEVONIAN

CARBONIFEROUS

PERMIAN

TRIASSIC

JURASSIC

CRETACEOUS

CENOZOIC

Name: *Placodus* (PLAK–oh–dus)
Order: Placodontia
Length: 3 m (10 ft)
Weight: 227 kg (500 lb)

ANIMAL PROFILE

Lystrosaurus

Lystrosaurus was a piglike paramammal with a pair of tusks and a shovel-like mouth. It was one of very few land animals that survived the Permian mas extinction and lived on into the Triassic period. It was also the most successful species ever. At one point, 95% of land vertebrates were *Lystrosaurus*.

Among other places, *Lystrosaurus* lived in Antarctica, but that land was not cold and icy at that time.

Global Survivor

The fossils of *Lystrosaurus* have been found in Africa, China, Antarctica, and Russia. This is evidence that all the landmasses were a single continent in the past, but have drifted apart since then. There are several theories as to why *Lystrosaurus* survived the great extinction. It may be because it could burrow and hibernate, or because it was partly aquatic, or because its broad diet meant that it could eat anything that had survived. Perhaps it flourished when all the meat-eating predators died out.

Fossil skin impressions show that *Lystrosaurus* had dimpled, leathery skin and was hairless.

250 MYA

CAMBRIAN	ORDOVICIAN	SILURIAN	DEVONIAN	CARBONIFEROUS	PERMIAN	TRIASSIC	JURASSIC	CRETACEOUS	CENOZOIC

Name: *Lystrosaurus*
(LIST–roh–SORE–us)
Clade: Therapsida
Length: 1 m (3.3 ft)
Weight: 90 kg (200 lb)

DINOSAUR PROFILE

DID YOU KNOW? The volcanic eruptions at the end of the Permian period wiped out 80% of all land creatures.

A Strange Mouth

Lystrosaurus belonged to the paramammal group called the dicynodonts. This means that they had two prominent doglike teeth in their mouths. These teeth are very obvious in *Lystrosaurus,* where they flank a broad, shovel-like beak. This mouth arrangement was suitable for digging in the ground for roots and tubers.

The long canine tusks were the only teeth *Lystrosaurus* had in its mouth.

Strong shoulders and front legs were good for digging. *Lystrosaurus* probably spent some of the time in burrows.

The legs of *Lystrosaurus* were partly splayed out at the side, like a reptile rather than a mammal.

Herrerasaurus

Dinosaurs did not appear until Triassic times. Throughout the Triassic, they had competition from many other kinds of land reptiles, some of which ran about on their hind legs. But the dinosaurs would develop unique features that made them the dominant kind of large animal on Earth—a dominance that would last for 165 million years.

The curved, bladed teeth of *Herrerasaurus* show that it was a meat-eating animal.

The First Dinosaurs

The earliest dinosaurs we know about come from Triassic rocks in Argentina. In a place called the Valley of the Moon, we find fossils of all kinds of animals, including these early dinosaurs. *Herrerasaurus* was a dinosaur—we can tell by the way the legs are joined to the hips and the hips to the backbone, and also by the arrangement of the ankle bones. However, it still had a very similar skull to many of the reptiles of Permian and earlier Triassic times.

Later, meat-eating theropod dinosaurs were built very much like the small early dinosaurs of Triassic South America. They evolved from animals like *Herrerasaurus*.

CAMBRIAN	ORDOVICIAN	SILURIAN	DEVONIAN	CARBONIFEROUS	PERMIAN	TRIASSIC	JURASSIC	CRETACEOUS	CENOZOIC

230 MYA

Name: *Herrerasaurus*
(HER–ray–rah–SORE–us)
Clade: Dinosauria
Length: 6 m (20 ft)
Weight: 350 kg (770 lb)

ANIMAL PROFILE

DID YOU KNOW? The first mammals lived at about the same time as *Herrerasaurus*.

The biggest animals on Earth traced their ancestors back to the smaller creatures of Triassic South America.

Big Descendants

The plant-eating dinosaurs that evolved from these early types were huge, went about on four legs, and had long necks and tiny heads. These were the sauropodomorphs. The later sauropodomorphs—the sauropods—lived in the Jurassic and Cretaceous periods. They became the biggest animals ever to walk the Earth.

The legs of *Herrerasaurus* were held vertically beneath the body, as in all later dinosaurs.

The hands with grasping claws and the palms facing one another are dinosaur features of *Herrerasaurus*.

Eoraptor

The desert rocks of the Valley of the Moon in Argentina were laid down in ancient, tropical riverside forests. They contain the fossils of many Triassic animals—big reptiles, small reptiles, primitive mammals, meat-eaters, and plant-eaters. Only about 6 percent of them are dinosaurs. The dinosaurs had not yet come to dominate the planet.

Small Hunter

The early dinosaur *Eoraptor* hunted some of the smallest animals in the forests. It was built just like the big meat-eating dinosaurs to come. It may have been the direct ancestor of the big meat-eaters, but some scientists think that it may have been an ancestor of the huge plant-eaters instead. There is always something new to be discovered in the study of fossils.

Eoraptor had sharp teeth for tearing prey.

Eoraptor had five fingers on each hand. Later theropods reduced them to three or even two.

DID YOU KNOW? The really big hunters in these forests were a kind of land-living crocodile. The early dinosaurs only hunted small lizards and mouse-like mammals.

Ferns and horsetail plants lined the banks of the rivers where *Eoraptor* hunted.

Other Evidence

It is not just fossil bones that tell us about what life was like millions of years ago. We often find fossils of footprints and trackways. These can show how an ancient animal moved, how fast it ran, how many lived in a group, and so on. Unfortunately, it is difficult to tell exactly which species made each fossil trackway.

Its legs show that *Eoraptor* was a strong runner. It hunted small, fast, nimble prey.

Fossil footprints from sandstones in Connecticut, USA, seem to match the feet of early dinosaurs like *Eoraptor*.

CAMBRIAN
ORDOVICIAN
SILURIAN
DEVONIAN
CARBONIFEROUS
PERMIAN
TRIASSIC
JURASSIC
CRETACEOUS
CENOZOIC

230 MYA

Name: *Eoraptor*
(EE-oh-RAP-tuhr)
Clade: Saurischia
Length: 1.7 m (5 ft 7 in)
Weight: 10 kg (22 lb)

ANIMAL PROFILE

Plateosaurus

The first big plant-eaters evolved in Triassic times. They were the long-necked sauropodomorphs. The earliest of these were relatively small and lightly built, and are sometimes called the prosauropods, because they came first. The biggest sauropods, like *Diplodocus* and *Brachiosaurus*, would evolve later, during the Jurassic and Cretaceous periods.

Dinosaur Graveyard

Dozens of skeletons of the Triassic sauropodomorph *Plateosaurus* have been found in sandstones in southern Germany. The animals had become trapped in the mud and quicksand of desert oases and were bogged down by their great weight. Because of the number of skeletons found, we know more about this animal than about any other dinosaur of the Triassic. We know it was a big-bodied plant-eater with a long neck.

Plateosaurus walked on its hind legs. It used its forelegs for reaching food.

210 MYA

CAMBRIAN	ORDOVICIAN	SILURIAN	DEVONIAN	CARBONIFEROUS	PERMIAN	TRIASSIC	JURASSIC	CRETACEOUS	CENOZOIC

Name: *Plateosaurus* (PLAT-ee-oh-SORE-us)
Clade: Sauropodomorpha
Length: 10 m (33 ft)
Weight: 4,000 kg (8,800 lb)

ANIMAL PROFILE

DID YOU KNOW? Many of the famous skeletons of *Plateosaurus* were destroyed when the museum in Berlin that housed them was bombed during World War II.

The long neck consisted of 10 vertebrae and was flexible enough to reach around branches for food.

The teeth of *Plateosaurus* were thick and leaf-shaped, with jagged edges like a vegetable grater.

The barrel-like body contained a huge digestive system. This would have been needed to break down and digest the tough desert plants of the time.

This old image of a *Plateosaurus* is wrong. Its wrist bones did not allow it to put its front feet flat on the ground like this.

How Did *Plateosaurus* Stand?

Plateosaurus had long, strong hind legs. The front legs were shorter but still strong. For a long time, we thought that it would sometimes go about on all fours like the later sauropods and sometimes on its hind legs like its ancestors. We now know that *Plateosaurus* could not have walked with all four feet on the ground.

Chapter 3

Warm, wet world

The Triassic period began with eruptions and extinctions. It ended with more extinctions caused by global warming, rising sea levels, and a wetter climate. Then came the Jurassic period, when sea reptiles, including ichthyosaurs like *Shonisaurus* (see page 28), and dinosaurs flourished. But the biggest swimmers were the plesiosaurs.

Two Types of Plesiosaurs

There were two types of plesiosaurs—the long-necked, small-headed plesiosauroids and the short-necked, big-headed pliosauroids. One of the biggest of the pliosauroids was *Liopleurodon*. Like a modern sperm whale, *Liopleurodon* ranged the oceans of the world, the biggest predator of the seas. It fed on big fish, squid-like cephalopods, and even other swimming reptiles with its long jaws and sharp teeth.

The teeth and jaws of *Liopleurodon* were strong enough to tackle the biggest animals in the ocean.

Liopleurodon was a typical pliosauroid.

Cryptoclidus, with its long neck and short head, was a typical plesiosauroid.

Spotter's Guide

The two types of plesiosaur are easy to tell apart. The pliosauroids had big heads with long jaws. The big head was separated from the body by a short thick neck. The plesiosauroids had tiny heads, with jaws full of sharp fish-catching teeth. The tiny head was separated from the body by a long neck. One early scientist thought that a plesiosauroid was like "a snake threaded through the body of a turtle"—but without a shell, of course.

DID YOU KNOW? The name *Liopleurodon* means "smooth–sided teeth." For a long time, only the fossil teeth of this animal were known.

CAMBRIAN
ORDOVICIAN
SILURIAN
DEVONIAN
CARBONIFEROUS
PERMIAN
TRIASSIC
JURASSIC
CRETACEOUS
CENOZOIC

165 MYA

Name: *Liopleurodon*
(LY–oh–PLOO–ro–don)
Order: Plesiosauria
Length: 10 m (33 ft)
Weight: 1.7 tonnes (1.85 tons)

ANIMAL PROFILE

Liopleurodon was the apex predator of the Jurassic seas. Nothing else around was as big and fierce as the giant pliosauroid.

The fingers and toes of a pliosaur were fused into a strong swimming paddle.

The big paddle limbs show that *Liopleurodon* would not have been able to swim fast for long periods, but it could lunge quickly in an ambush attack.

47

Geosaurus

One branch of the crocodile family took to the seas in Jurassic times. These were a group called the thalattosuchians—the ocean crocodiles. There were two families of these: the teleosauroids, which kept their basic crocodile shape, and the metriorhynchoids, which were more highly adapted to life in the ocean.

Adapted to Sea Life

Geosaurus was a typical metriorhynchoid. It had paddles instead of legs and a fishlike fin on the end of its tail. It never ventured out onto land. Like the other sea reptiles of the Jurassic period, the ichthyosaurs and the plesiosaurs, its ancestors had given up life on land altogether.

Geosaurus may have hunted by suction—opening its jaws so suddenly that water was sucked into the mouth, carrying prey with it.

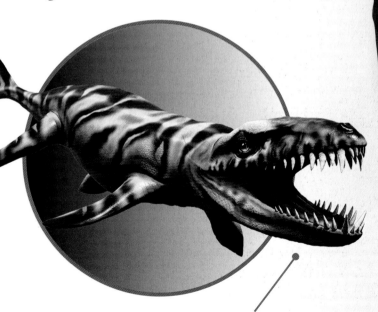

Dakosaurus, a 5 m (16 ft) long metriorhynchoid with a huge head, was nicknamed "Godzilla" when its fossil was found.

The biggest species of *Geosaurus* took over from *Liopleurodon* (see page 46) as the apex marine predator at the end of the Jurassic.

Land and Sea

The other group of thalattosuchians, the teleosauroids, would have been able to spend some time on land. They still had legs, feet, and toes, although these were very short and were held tight to the side of the body while swimming in the sea. With their long, narrow fish-catching jaws, they looked a bit like the modern gharial crocodile but were only distantly related.

Statues of *Teleosaurus* were built for the first prehistoric theme park in Crystal Palace, London, in 1854.

Geosaurus had smooth skin without the bony plates we see in a modern crocodile.

150 MYA

CAMBRIAN	ORDOVICIAN	SILURIAN	DEVONIAN	CARBONIFEROUS	PERMIAN	TRIASSIC	JURASSIC	CRETACEOUS	CENOZOIC

Name: *Geosaurus*
(JEE-oh-SAWR-us)
Superorder:
  Crocodylomorphia
Length: 3 m (10 ft)
Weight: 80 kg (180 lb)

ANIMAL PROFILE

DID YOU KNOW? Different species of *Geosaurus* had different-sized teeth depending on what they ate—squid, fish, or other swimming reptiles.

Rhamphorhynchus

After the gliding reptiles of the Triassic (see page 32) and before the birds appeared (see page 66), the skies belonged to the flying reptiles—the pterosaurs. Pterosaurs were not dinosaurs, but they did belong to the same family, along with the crocodiles and the birds. They ruled the skies from Late Triassic times until the great extinction at the end of the Cretaceous period.

The wing of *Rhamphorhynchus*—and all other pterosaurs—was held out by an enormous fourth finger. The finger bones were as long as arm bones.

Wing Fingers

Pterosaurs were active, warm-blooded flying reptiles, with furry bodies and leathery wings that were supported by a very long, strong fourth finger. The earlier types, such as *Rhamphorhynchus*, had long tails and narrow wings. Later types had broader wings and short tails. Like modern birds, they came in all shapes and sizes, with different-shaped heads and jaws, depending on what they ate. *Rhamphorhynchus* fed on fish.

While on the ground, a pterosaur walked on all fours. It took to the air in a jump. We can tell this from fossil footprints.

CAMBRIAN	ORDOVICIAN	SILURIAN	DEVONIAN	CARBONIFEROUS	PERMIAN	TRIASSIC	JURASSIC	CRETACEOUS	CENOZOIC

150 MYA

Name: *Rhamphorhynchus* (RAM–foh–RINK–us)
Order: Pterosauria
Wingspan: 1.8 m (5 ft 10in)
Weight: 0.9 kg (2 lb)

ANIMAL PROFILE

DID YOU KNOW? The best fossils of *Rhamphorhynchus* have been found in a quarry in southern Germany. Even the skin of the wing is fossilized.

The sharp teeth of *Rhamphorhynchus* show that it ate fish, catching them as it skimmed above the surface of the water.

Two Types

The two types of pterosaur were the rhamphorhynchoids and the pterodactyloids. The rhamphorhynchoids came first and lasted until the end of the Jurassic. Then they were replaced by the pterodactyloids. By the end of the Cretaceous period, the pterodactyloids became the biggest animals ever to fly.

Rhamphorhynchoids had narrow wings, a short neck, and a long tail with a vane used for steering.

Pterodactyloids had broad wings, a long neck, and no tail.

Coelophysis

By the start of the Jurassic period, dinosaurs were developing into the different types that would walk the Earth until the end of the Cretaceous period. There were the meat-eating theropods, the long-necked, plant-eating sauropods, and the various types of plant-eating ornithischians.

Nimble Hunter

Most of the small carnivorous dinosaurs of the latest Triassic and earliest Jurassic periods looked like *Coelophysis*. They had a small, slim body, long running legs, head held out at the front on a long neck, and nimble grasping hands. Although *Coelophysis* itself was found in North America, the fossils of very similar theropods have been found in South Africa.

By the end of the Triassic and early Jurassic periods, dinosaurs were beginning to take over from land–living crocodiles as the main predators of the time.

Flood Victims

The most famous *Coelophysis* fossils were found in New Mexico, where a whole pack of them perished in a flood and their skeletons were perfectly preserved. Usually, dinosaur fossils consist only of scattered pieces of bone. A full dinosaur skeleton, with the bones still joined together, is very rare.

The *Coelophysis* skeletons were covered by sand very quickly. This helped preserve them.

CAMBRIAN
ORDOVICIAN
SILURIAN
DEVONIAN
CARBONIFEROUS
PERMIAN
TRIASSIC
JURASSIC
CRETACEOUS
CENOZOIC

215
MYA

Name: *Coelophysis*
(SEE–loh–FISE–iss)
Clade: Theropoda
Length: 3 m (10 ft)
Weight: 25 kg (55 lb)

ANIMAL
PROFILE

Coelophysis lived
on riverbanks in
open, arid plains that
were periodically
swept by floods.

Did *Coelophysis*
live in herds? Or
were the bodies in
New Mexico just
washed together by
the flood? We are
still not sure.

DID YOU KNOW? A skull fossil of *Coelophysis*
was taken into space on the space shuttle in 1998.

53

Dilophosaurus

As the Jurassic period continued, more and more meat-eating dinosaurs appeared. These all belonged to a group called the theropods, and they all had a similar shape—they walked on two legs, with a mouthful of teeth held out at the front, balanced by a heavy tail.

The teeth could tackle any meat, from big animals, small animals, or even carrion (animals already dead).

Meat-Eaters Get Bigger

Dilophosaurus was one of the earliest of the big theropods. It was not as huge as the great monsters to come, but it was certainly the fiercest animal around at the time. With its sharp teeth and strong claws, it was built to attack animals bigger than itself. However, it would also have hunted smaller things and would even have eaten animals that had already died.

The teeth were longer and more blade-like on the upper jaw than on the lower jaw.

193 MYA

Name: *Dilophosaurus*
(dy–LOFF–oh–SORE–us)
Clade: Theropoda
Height: 4 m (13 ft)
Length: 7 m (23 ft)
Weight: 400 kg (880 lb)

ANIMAL PROFILE

The body of *Dilophosaurus* was as heavy as the largest black bear ever recorded.

Fossil impressions around one individual suggest that *Dilophosaurus* had feathers, but not all scientists agree.

Dilophosaurus had a lightly built skull. The front part was articulated so that it could twitch, probably to prise small animals out of rock crevices.

Show-Off!

Dilophosaurus had two crests running down the top of its head. These were too thin to have been weapons of any sort. They must have been used for display— to show off to rivals or to attract mates. They would probably have been patterned in bright hues to make them easily recognizable.

DID YOU KNOW? There is a *Dilophosaurus* in the film *Jurassic Park*, but the filmmakers got it all wrong. It was too small, had imaginary neck decorations, and spat poison!

55

Yangchuanosaurus

The really big meat-eating theropods of the Jurassic period are what we call the carnosaurs. They ranged from the enormous *Allosaurus* of North America and the huge *Carcharodontosaurus* of Africa, to the great *Yangchuanosaurus* of China. The long-necked, plant-eating sauropods of the time were their prey.

Dragon from China

Yangchuanosaurus, like the other carnosaurs, used its strong claws and its vicious teeth for killing. It ran at great speeds, powered by the huge muscles of its hind legs. Its clawed hands could sink into the flesh of its prey. The muscles of its neck could bring down the open mouth with the force of a steam hammer. Then, the blade-like teeth could rip out chunks of meat.

Yangchuanosaurus had several little horns over its eyes and a ridge of bone on the nose.

The sharp teeth were replaced all the time as they wore out.

Another carnosaur, *Cryolophosaurus,* had a tall crest above its eyes. Its fossils were found in Antarctica.

The carnosaurs may have hunted in packs to kill the biggest animals they could.

A Mysterious Animal

The carnosaur *Megalosaurus* was the first dinosaur to have been discovered and named, back in 1827. Nobody knew what a dinosaur looked like then. The only fossils known were a jawbone with teeth and some hipbones. They were thought to have belonged to some kind of giant lizard. Scientists imagined that it looked like a four-footed dragon.

A statue of *Megalosaurus*, as it was then thought to have looked, stands in the grounds of Crystal Palace Park in London, UK.

159 MYA

| CAMBRIAN | ORDOVICIAN | SILURIAN | DEVONIAN | CARBONIFEROUS | PERMIAN | TRIASSIC | JURASSIC | CRETACEOUS | CENOZOIC |

Name: *Yangchuanosaurus*
(YANG–koo–an–oh–SAWR–us)
Clade: Theropoda
Length: 8 m (26 ft)
Weight: 3 tonnes (3.3 tons)

ANIMAL PROFILE

DID YOU KNOW? The first skeleton of *Yangchuanosaurus* was found in 1977 by workers building a dam in China.

Diplodocus

The biggest of the Jurassic plant-eaters were the long-necked sauropods. They became the biggest land-living animals ever. In Jurassic times, they developed into two major groups—the diplodocids, which were long and low, and the macronarians, which were tall, but not as long. The most famous of the diplodocids was *Diplodocus* itself.

Dinosaur Celebrity

An almost complete fossil of *Diplodocus* was unearthed in 1899 in Wyoming, USA, by an expedition funded by Scottish-American steel tycoon Andrew Carnegie. Once the skeleton was assembled in his museum in Pittsburgh, Carnegie was so pleased with it that he had plaster casts made of all 300 bones, so that he could send copies of the skeleton to the museums of several capital cities throughout the world. As a result, in the early twentieth century, *Diplodocus* was the best known of all dinosaurs.

Like the hose on a vacuum cleaner, the long neck could gather things up from a broad area without *Diplodocus* needing to move the bulk of its body very much.

The skull of *Diplodocus* was as big as that of a horse. But it was small compared to *Diplodocus'* body.

Its teeth were like the teeth of a comb. They could rake twigs and leaves from the branches and stalks of low-growing plants.

DID YOU KNOW? A partial skeleton of a sauropod that may have been 33 m (110 ft) long was found in 1991 and named *Seismosaurus*. It is now thought to be a species of *Diplodocus*.

A Long Reach

The neck of *Diplodocus* consisted of at least 15 vertebrae and was 6.5 m (21 ft) long, reaching forward almost horizontally from the shoulders. It could swing its neck from side to side in a broad arc, reaching low-growing plants in front of it and at each side.

Because the body was well balanced at the hips, *Diplodocus* could also reach up on is hind legs to feed from high branches.

The long, narrow tail consisted of 82 bones. It was used as a whip against any predators.

153 MYA

CAMBRIAN	ORDOVICIAN	SILURIAN	DEVONIAN	CARBONIFEROUS	PERMIAN	TRIASSIC	JURASSIC	CRETACEOUS	CENOZOIC

Name: *Diplopdocus*
(dip–LOH–doh–kus)
Clade: Sauropoda
Length: 26 m (85 ft)
Weight: 14 tonnes
(16 tons)

ANIMAL PROFILE

Brachiosaurus

The second sauropod group were the macronarians. While the diplodocids had long bodies, the macronarians were remarkably tall. Unusually for dinosaurs, their forelegs were longer than their hind legs, and their shoulders were very tall. This allowed them to reach up into the highest trees to browse on leaves, needles, and twigs.

The skull of *Brachiosaurus* has a huge space in the nose area, giving the head a domed appearance. Macronarian means "big nosed."

The Towering Giant

Brachiosaurus was the first macronarian to be discovered. Because scientists of the time didn't have enough information, when fossils of other macronarians were found, they were named *Brachiosaurus* as well. Now we know that many of these discoveries were closely related to *Brachiosaurus,* but were actually different enough to be different species. *Brachiosaurus* lived alongside *Diplodocus* and the other diplodocids in North America at the end of the Jurassic period.

This vast macronarian in the Berlin museum was once thought to be *Brachiosaurus*. It is now known to be *Giraffatitan*.

CAMBRIAN	ORDOVICIAN	SILURIAN	DEVONIAN	CARBONIFEROUS	PERMIAN	TRIASSIC	JURASSIC	CRETACEOUS	CENOZOIC

150 MYA

Name: *Brachiosaurus* (BRAK-ee-oh-SORE-us)
Clade: Sauropoda
Length: 22 m (72 ft)
Weight: 47 tonnes (52 tons)

ANIMAL PROFILE

A Long-Lived Family

The macronarians appeared in the middle of the Jurassic period and survived until the very end of the age of dinosaurs, at the end of the Cretaceous period. During that time, they spread throughout the world and developed many strange shapes.

The macronarian *Camarasaurus* was the most common dinosaur of North America in the late Jurassic.

Europasaurus: a dwarf macronarian, the size of a cow, that lived on Jurassic islands.

The tail of *Brachiosaurus* was quite short. It was used to balance the movement of the neck and head.

The legs were held straight and pillar-like to support the great weight of the animal.

DID YOU KNOW? A vertebra from the backbone of *Brachiosaurus* would have been as as long as an 8-year-old child.

Camptosaurus

Besides the sauropods, the other major group of the plant-eating dinosaurs was a group that we call the ornithopods—the "bird-footed." The sauropods supported their big plant-eating bodies on all fours. The ornithopods could balance their heavy bodies in a different way, and so most of them could walk on their hind legs.

Like other ornithopods, *Camptosaurus* had a beak at the front of its mouth with cheeks at each side to hold plant material while it chewed.

A Fast Plant-Eater

Camptosaurus was a common ornithopod in the late Jurassic period. It usually walked on its hind legs and kept its hands free, so that it could gather food. Its food was any plant material it could reach and, judging by the wear on its tightly packed teeth, was quite tough. Since it had strong hind legs, it could run away from the big meat-eaters of the time, such as the carnosaurs (see page 56).

Dryosaurus was a small, ostrich-sized ornithopod, that lived alongside *Camptosaurus*.

Pigeon-Toed

The term "bird-footed" comes from the arrangement of the bones of the foot. In the 1800s, scientists thought they were like those of a bird. This distinguished them from the sauropods, in which the toes were thought to have been like the toes of a lizard, or the theropods, in which they were believed to be like the toes of a mammal.

An ornithopod's footprint has three toes. *Camptosaurus* also had a fourth, rear claw.

The big plant-eating gut of *Camptosaurus* was held below its hips, so the animal could balance on its hind legs.

Camptosaurus' hand had five fingers. It was used for grabbing food and sometimes for walking.

150 MYA

CAMBRIAN

ORDOVICIAN

SILURIAN

DEVONIAN

CARBONIFEROUS

PERMIAN

TRIASSIC

JURASSIC

CRETACEOUS

CENOZOIC

Name: *Camptosasurus*
(KAMP–toe–SORE–us)
Clade: Ornithopoda
Length: 7.9 m (26 ft)
Weight: 800 kg (1,760 lb)

ANIMAL PROFILE

DID YOU KNOW? *Camptosaurus* could probably run at 25 kph (15 mph).

Stegosaurus

The thyreophorans were the dinosaurs protected by shields and plates. The stegosaurs were those that had plates on their backs and spikes on their tails. The plates were arranged vertically and ran in two rows down the neck, back, and tail.

The plates had a bony core and were covered with either skin or horn.

The Biggest and Showiest

With a double row of vertical plates down its back, two pairs of spikes on the end of its tail, and a tiny head, *Stegosaurus* is one of the most recognizable dinosaurs. It was the biggest of the stegosaur group— as long as a tenniscourt is wide. From the side, it would have looked even bigger, with the huge plates towering above the line of its back.

We have found many good fossils of *Stegosaurus*, so we know a lot about its skeleton.

Different Styles

All the stegosaurs had a double row of plates down the back and spikes on the tail, but the arrangement of plates and spikes differed between individual species. The first stegosaurs appeared in the area of China in the middle Jurassic period. From there, they spread to the rest of the world. They all died out by the middle of the Cretaceous, and their place was taken by the ankylosaurs.

Miragaia was a late Jurassic stegosaur from Portugal, with a long neck like a sauropod.

Kentrosaurus, from late Jurassic East Africa, had more spines than plates. Its plates were small and narrow.

If the plates were covered in skin, they would have been used for heat regulation. If covered in horn, they would have been used for protection.

Sharp spines stuck out at the sides of the tail tip. The tail could be swung at an enemy with force, causing terrible damage.

CAMBRIAN	ORDOVICIAN	SILURIAN	DEVONIAN	CARBONIFEROUS	PERMIAN	TRIASSIC	JURASSIC	CRETACEOUS	CENOZOIC

● 150 MYA

Name: *Stegosaurus*
(STEG–oh–SORE–us)
Clade: Thyreophora
Length: 7 m (23 ft)
Weight: 3.8 tonnes
(4.2 tons)

ANIMAL PROFILE

DID YOU KNOW? Scientists used to think that *Stegosaurus* had a second brain in its hips to control its hind legs and tail. In fact, the space in the hips probably contained a reserve of glycogen—a source of extra energy.

Archaeopteryx

These days, the birds rule the skies—but back in the Jurassic period, the pterosaurs filled the air. The birds were just beginning to appear at that time. They developed from small theropod meat-eating dinosaurs. Many scientists regard birds as actual surviving dinosaurs!

The feathers on the arms of *Archaeopteryx* had the same shape and the same overlapping pattern as on the wings of a modern flying bird. *Archaeopteryx* was a true flier.

Early Bird

Archaeopteryx is widely regarded as being the first bird. It had the bony tail, clawed hands, and toothy jaw of a small dinosaur, but it also had the wings and feathers of a bird. When its fossils were first discovered in the 1860s, they were used as proof that one kind of animal could evolve from another. *Archaeopteryx* was not alone—at that time, other dinosaurs also developed birdlike features.

Microraptor had flight feathers on its arms, legs, and tail. This small dinosaur could glide from tree to tree.

CAMBRIAN	ORDOVICIAN	SILURIAN	DEVONIAN	CARBONIFEROUS	PERMIAN	TRIASSIC	JURASSIC	CRETACEOUS	CENOZOIC

240 MYA

Name: *Archaeopteryx* (ARK–ee–OPT–er–ix)
Clade: Theropoda
Length: 50 cm (1 ft 8 in)
Weight: 1 kg (0.82 lb)

ANIMAL PROFILE

DID YOU KNOW? *Archaeopteryx* is known from a dozen fossils, all found in the same quarry in southern Germany.

Iberomesornis could fly with its clawed wings. It had a more birdlike tail than *Archaeopteryx*.

Part Bird, Part Dinosaur

Feathers first appeared on small Jurassic theropods as insulation to keep the animal warm. It was only later that these feathers developed other purposes. Some feathers became big and showy, and were used for display. Sometimes, these showy feathers could be used to catch the wind and help the animal run faster. Eventually, these became flight feathers.

Caudipteryx had showy feathers on its arms—not quite wings— and could not fly.

Later birds had a beak instead of jaws and teeth, lost their wing claws, and developed a stubby tail—all of which made them lighter than *Archaeopteryx* and helped them fly better.

Chapter 4

Dinosaurs rule

The Cretaceous period saw a great flourishing of life. Marine reptiles, dinosaurs, mammals, and flowering plants spread across the shallow seas and the ice-free land. The dinosaurs were the mightiest of all. By this time, there were also many types of birds, but the pterosaurs still ruled the skies.

Flying Dragon

With a wingspan as wide as a small plane, *Quetzalcoatlus* was the first of the gigantic pterosaurs to be discovered by paleontologists. It belonged to a pterosaur group called the azhdarchids, which were all huge. They probably hunted on the ground. When they stood on land, *Quetzalcoatlus* and the other azhdarchids like *Hatzegopteryx* were as tall as a modern giraffe.

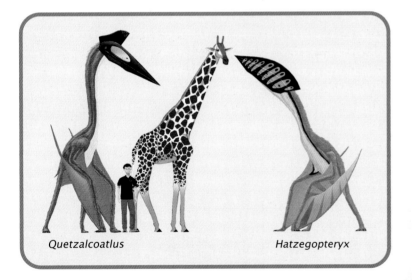

Quetzalcoatlus   Hatzegopteryx

The arms of *Quetzalcoatlus* worked as wings in flight. They were also strong enough to support the whole animal while walking on the ground.

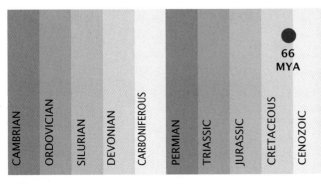

66 MYA

CAMBRIAN | ORDOVICIAN | SILURIAN | DEVONIAN | CARBONIFEROUS | PERMIAN | TRIASSIC | JURASSIC | CRETACEOUS | CENOZOIC

Name: *Quetzalcoatlus*
(KWETS-ul-koh-AT-lus)
Order: Pterosauria
Wingspan: 12 m (39 ft)
Weight: 250 kg (550 lb)

ANIMAL PROFILE

DID YOU KNOW? *Quetzalcoatlus* would have spent more of its time on the ground than in the air.

Its jaws show that *Quetzalcoatlus* did not catch fish like many other pterosaurs did, but hunted small ground-living animals after landing.

The wings may have contained air sacs, joined to the lungs, which would help *Quetzalcoatlus* breathe.

Look at Me!

Each of the big pterosaurs had a differently shaped head and jaw, depending on the food it ate. Each species also had a different gaudily patterned crest, so that they could be recognized by others of the same species— just like bright feathers on modern birds.

Pterodaustro filtered tiny pond animals with its comblike jaws.

Tapejara had a crest of skin stretched between bony struts.

Long-crested *Thalassodromeus* had a skull as lightweight as polystyrene.

Jakapil

The big, shield-bearing thyreophoran dinosaurs like *Stegosaurus* (see page 64) and *Ankylosaurus* (see page 88) are well known, but there were many small types as well. Most small thyreophorans lived in Triassic and early Jurassic times. Some, like *Jakapil*, survived into the Cretaceous period.

A Tough Little Beast

Jakapil was covered all over in small shields that protected its head, its back, and its limbs. Fossils were found in Argentina, the first time that the remains of a small thyreophoran had been found there, showing that these animals spread all over the world.

The fact that *Jakapil* had tiny forelimbs compared with its longer rear limbs shows us that it went around on two feet.

Other small thyreophorans, such as *Scutellosaurus*, lived about 100 million years earlier than *Jakapil*.

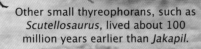

								95 MYA ●	
CAMBRIAN	ORDOVICIAN	SILURIAN	DEVONIAN	CARBONIFEROUS	PERMIAN	TRIASSIC	JURASSIC	CRETACEOUS	CENOZOIC

Name: *Jakapil*
  (JAK–a–pil)
Clade: Thyreophora
Length: 1.5 m (4.9 ft)
Weight: 7 kg (15.4 lb)

ANIMAL PROFILE

Keep Out!

The later thyreophorans had shields like flat plates arranged lengthways down their bodies, but in the early forms, the shields tended to be small and simple in shape. The weight of the shields meant that the biggest of these animals went about on four feet, but the smallest, including *Jakapil*, were light enough to be two-footed.

Jakapil even had little shields on its face. The shields consisted of bone covered in horn.

The teeth of *Jakapil* show that it was able to chew its food, unlike the bigger thyreophorans who just chopped it and swallowed.

Jakapil lived in the damp oasis areas of a huge desert.

DID YOU KNOW? *Jakapil* is one of very few thyreophoran dinosaurs that have been found in the southern hemisphere.

Ichthyovenator

The big, meat-eating theropod dinosaurs usually hunted and ate other big dinosaurs. However, in Cretaceous times, there existed a group of very large theropods called the spinosaurs. They lived beside rivers and fed on fish. We can tell because scientists have found fish remains in the stomach contents of their fossil skeletons.

Big Sailbacks

Most of the spinosaurs that we know about had sails on their backs, supported by a fence of bony struts sticking up from their backbones. These were probably used for signaling or adjusting their body temperature (like *Dimetrodon*, see page 22) or for helping to swim—we are not quite sure. *Ichthyovenator* was different from the others as its sail was divided in two. Part of it was on the back, and part was on the tail.

The long jaws and pointed teeth of *Ichthyovenator* were like those of a fish-eating crocodile.

At 14 m (46 ft) long, *Spinosaurus* was the biggest of the spinosaurs. It was also the longest of all the meat eating theropods.

The best spinosaur skeleton known is of *Baryonyx* but does not appear to have had a sail. However, the vertebrae seem to have had their spines broken off. Perhaps the sail broke off before it was fossilized.

Amphibious Dinosaur

We think that *Ichthyovenator* and the other spinosaurs lived in or near the water, because their bones had the same chemical composition that we find in water-living crocodiles and turtles. Some of the bones were quite heavy, which would have helped to control their buoyancy.

The eyes and nostrils were high up on the skull, so it could dip its snout into water to catch fish.

The thumb of a spinosaur had a big hooked claw, possibly for hooking fish.

120 MYA

Name: *Ichthyovenator*
(ik–thee–ov–en–ah–tor)
Clade: Theropoda
Length: 10 m (34 ft)
Weight: 2.4 tonnes (2.6 tons)

ANIMAL PROFILE

CAMBRIAN
ORDOVICIAN
SILURIAN
DEVONIAN
CARBONIFEROUS
PERMIAN
TRIASSIC
JURASSIC
CRETACEOUS
CENOZOIC

DID YOU KNOW? *Ichthyovenator* was one of the smallest of the spinosaurs.

Dakotaraptor

Some of the fiercest meat-eating theropod dinosaurs were the dromaeosaurids—the "running reptiles." These were usually small, like the famous *Velociraptor,* and hunted swift-running prey through the undergrowth. But during the Cretaceous period, some of these, such as *Dakotaraptor*, became very large.

The big animals of the Cretaceous plains may have had nothing to fear from *Dakotaraptor*. It would have gone for smaller prey.

Wings, but Flying Nowhere

The fossil arm bones of *Dakotaraptor* show where long feathers were attached. However, these must have been used for showing off or controlling the animal's steering while running. With a body as big as a bear, *Dakotaraptor* was too heavy to fly. It lived in the same time and place as *Tyrannosaurus,* but the two great beasts must have hunted different prey— *Tyrannosaurus* hunted big, slow animals by ambush, while *Dakotaraptor* chased down its food.

Chicken-sized *Mononykus* was a small cretaceous theropod with a single strong claw on each hand. It probably ate ants and termites.

66 MYA

Name: *Dakotaraptor*
(DA–coh–ta–RAP–tuhr)
Clade: Theropoda
Length: 5.5 m (18 ft)
Weight: 350 kg (772 lb)

ANIMAL PROFILE

CAMBRIAN	ORDOVICIAN	SILURIAN	DEVONIAN	CARBONIFEROUS	PERMIAN	TRIASSIC	JURASSIC	CRETACEOUS	CENOZOIC

A Loving Family of Killers

The dromaeosaurids, including *Dakotaraptor*, probably laid their eggs in nests, incubated them, and looked after their young when they hatched—very much like their descendants the birds do. We can deduce this because we have found fossils of the nests and young of similar small meat-eating dinosaurs.

This oviraptor mother on a nest spreads out her wing and tail feathers to help incubate her eggs.

Like its smaller dromaeosaurid relatives, *Dakotaraptor* had a huge killing claw on its second toe.

The flapping wings of *Dakotaraptor* would have helped it balance while fighting and subduing its prey.

DID YOU KNOW? *Dakotaraptor* was one of the last of the dromaeosaurids. It lived at the very end of the Cretaceous period.

75

Deinocheirus

For 50 years, the fossil remains of a big dinosaur from Mongolia puzzled scientists. All they had was a pair of arms and hands with the most enormous fingers and claws ever seen. There were all kinds of guesses about the owner of these limbs, but nobody had any idea of just how odd the whole animal was.

What a Strange Beast!

When a pair of almost complete skeletons of this animal were eventually found, scientists realized that it was not just the hands that were strange. Despite being a theropod, it had the massive body and duck-like jaws of a plant-eater. The huge claws were probably used for tearing down vegetation. They determined that it belonged to a theropod group called the ornithomimids—which are usually quite elegant and lightweight animals. But not *Deinocheirus*!

A typical ornithomimid, such as *Gallimimus*, was an elegant, fleet-footed, ostrich-sized theropod.

More Big Hands

Another dinosaur group with big hands were the therizinosaurs. These were also theropods, but while most other theropods ate meat, therizinosaurs actually ate plants. They may have used their long fingers with enormous scythe-like claws to pull down branches and rip off the leaves for food. The scythelike claws may also have been used for display, to frighten off enemies or to attract mates.

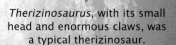

Therizinosaurus, with its small head and enormous claws, was a typical therizinosaur.

DID YOU KNOW? Although the arms were discovered in 1965, the rest of the skeleton of *Deinocheirus* was not found until 2014.

CAMBRIAN

ORDOVICIAN

SILURIAN

DEVONIAN

CARBONIFEROUS

PERMIAN

TRIASSIC

JURASSIC

CRETACEOUS

CENOZOIC

Name: *Deinocheirus*
(dy–no–KY–rus)
Clade: Theropoda
Length: 11 m (36 ft)
Weight: 2 tonnes (2.2 tons)

ANIMAL
PROFILE

The skull was long and flat, like that of duckbilled dinosaurs (see page 84). But it had no teeth in its deep lower jaw.

Deinocheirus had tall spines over its hips to support some kind of hump.

Like the other ornithomimids, *Deinocheirus* was warm–blooded and covered in feathers.

Tyrannosaurus

The tyrannosaurids were one of the last meat-eating theropod groups to evolve. Although they started as small animals in Jurassic times, they later developed into the largest land-living meat-eaters that ever lived. They dominated the continents of Asia and North America at the end of the Cretaceous.

Terrifying Hunter

The last of the meat-eating dinosaurs is probably the best known. *Tyrannosaurus*, often given its full name *Tyrannosaurus rex*, was not only the last but one of the biggest. It had huge, teeth-filled jaws in a heavy skull. It could focus its eyes on prey in front of it—a useful skill in hunting. Its ears were attuned to the sounds that animals make while walking on the ground— useful while waiting in ambush.

The young *Tyrannosaurus* was like a different animal—feathered, long-jawed, small-bodied, and swift-footed. It hunted a different kind of prey from its parent.

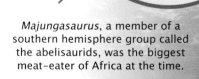

Majungasaurus, a member of a southern hemisphere group called the abelisaurids, was the biggest meat-eater of Africa at the time.

The Biggest Meat-Eaters

It was not just *Tyrannosaurus* and its relatives that grew larger at the end of the Cretaceous. The theropod families on other continents developed huge forms as well, some of them almost reaching the size of *Tyrannosaurus*.

Megaraptor, a kind of carnosaur (see page 56), was the biggest meat-eater in South America in the late Cretaceous.

Tyrannosaurus had small, gripping teeth at the front of its mouth; blade-like, meat-shearing teeth farther back; and stout, bone-crunching teeth at the back.

Its strong hind legs were not for long-distance running, but for sprinting out of cover in an ambush.

66 MYA

CAMBRIAN	ORDOVICIAN	SILURIAN	DEVONIAN	CARBONIFEROUS	PERMIAN	TRIASSIC	JURASSIC	CRETACEOUS	CENOZOIC

Name: *Tyrannosaurus*
(ty–RAN–oh–SORE–us)
Clade: Theropoda
Length: 12.4 m (40 ft)
Weight: 8.7 tonnes (9.8 tons)

ANIMAL PROFILE

DID YOU KNOW? *Tyrannosaurus* had the strongest bite force of any land-living animal.

Alamosaurus

Nature saved the biggest until last! The sauropod group called the titanosaurs lived at the very end of the Cretaceous period and included the biggest animals ever to live on dry land. They were part of the macronarian line, like Jurassic *Brachiosaurus* (see page 60).

Each neck bone of *Alamosaurus* consisted of struts and flat plates, arranged to make a lightweight structure with great strength.

Mountains of Flesh and Bone

The biggest of the titanosaurs have been found in South America, but *Alamosaurus* was the largest species in North America. It probably migrated from the south when a land bridge emerged between the two continents. There had been no sauropods in North America for the previous 30 million years, since early Cretaceous times.

Many species of titanosaur, such as *Saltasaurus*, had protective bony plates in the skin of their backs.

68 MYA

Name: *Alamosaurus*
(ah–LAH–mow–SORE–us)
Clade: Sauropoda
Length: 30 m (100 ft)
Weight: 80 tonnes (88 tons)

ANIMAL PROFILE

CAMBRIAN	ORDOVICIAN	SILURIAN	DEVONIAN	CARBONIFEROUS	PERMIAN	TRIASSIC	JURASSIC	CRETACEOUS	CENOZOIC

DID YOU KNOW? Titanosaur remains have been found on all seven continents, including Antarctica.

Why So Big?

The sheer size of the titanosaurs is difficult to imagine. We can only get the idea by seeing a diagram of one, such as *Patagotitan*, beside a human figure.

The titanosaurs were not the only animals to grow large, although they were the largest. The theropods (see page 52) and the crocodiles (see page 92) also grew bigger toward the end of the Cretaceous.

We do not know why. A changing climate and new types of vegetation might have been part of the cause.

Alamosaurus was not fussy about its diet. Fossilized stomach contents contain all kinds of plants in the area at that time.

Titanosaurs had no toes. Their hand and foot bones had turned into vertical columns to support the great weight.

Iguanodon

There were plenty of ornithopods in the Jurassic period (see page 62), but it was during the Cretaceous that they really came into their own. Toward the end of the period, they developed into a group called the duckbills. They were the most varied and abundant plant-eaters of the time.

Plant-Eating Reptile

One of the most famous of the ornithopods, and one of the first dinosaurs to be discovered, was from the earliest part of the Cretaceous period. The first fossils found were of teeth, and these seemed to come from a big plant-eating reptile. They were like those of the modern plant-eating iguana lizard, so the animal was given the name *Iguanodon*— "iguana tooth."

Iguanodon walked on all fours, but could raise itself on its big hind legs to feed from trees. Its hands could be used for both walking and grasping.

The Duckbills

A group of ornithopods called the duckbills developed from animals like *Iguanodon*. They take their name from the beak at the front of the mouth, which became broad and flat like a duck's beak. The many types of duckbills spread all across the world at the end of the Cretaceous period.

Many duckbills, like *Olorotitan*, developed big, strange-shaped crests on the tops of their heads.

DID YOU KNOW? About 40 skeletons of *Iguanodon* were found together in a coal mine in Belgium in 1878.

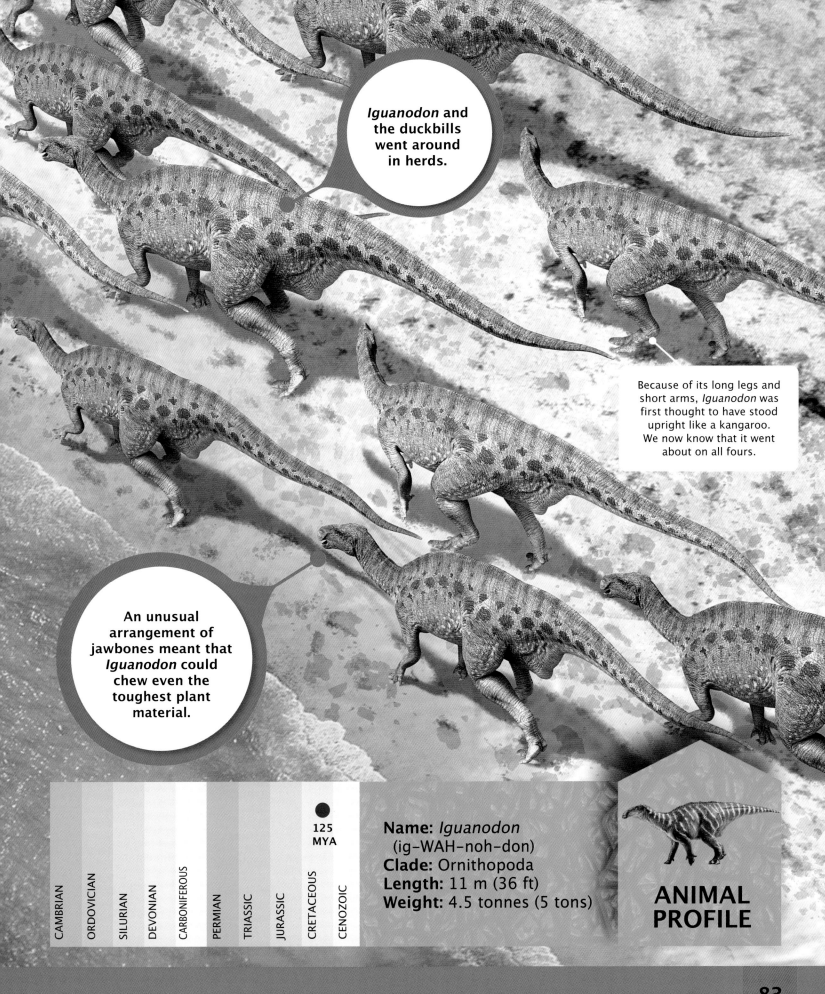

Iguanodon and the duckbills went around in herds.

Because of its long legs and short arms, *Iguanodon* was first thought to have stood upright like a kangaroo. We now know that it went about on all fours.

An unusual arrangement of jawbones meant that *Iguanodon* could chew even the toughest plant material.

125 MYA

CAMBRIAN
ORDOVICIAN
SILURIAN
DEVONIAN
CARBONIFEROUS
PERMIAN
TRIASSIC
JURASSIC
CRETACEOUS
CENOZOIC

Name: *Iguanodon* (ig–WAH–noh–don)
Clade: Ornithopoda
Length: 11 m (36 ft)
Weight: 4.5 tonnes (5 tons)

ANIMAL PROFILE

Triceratops

The ceratopsians were horned dinosaurs. Like most groups, they started as small rabbit-sized animals. By the end of the Cretaceous, they were huge horned monsters, with massive shields around their necks and horns on their faces.

The Biggest Ceratopsian

The last of the ceratopsians was three-horned *Triceratops*. It looked a little like a rhinoceros, but with a frill around its neck; two long, forward-pointing horns above the eyes; and a smaller horn on the snout. It lived in huge herds on the plains of today's North America.

Triceratops used its horns to defend against attacks from big meat–eaters like *Tyrannosaurus* (see page 80).

Other Ceratopsians

Toward the end of the Cretaceous period, many types of ceratopsian appeared. Each had a similar body, but a different arrangement of horns and frills on the head.

Centrosaurus

Einiosaurus

Styracosaurus

Nasutoceratops

Diabloceratops

The horns of *Triceratops* were covered in a keratin sheath like the horns of a goat. They kept growing throughout the animal's life.

The neck shield protected the neck and the shoulders—useful when two males were sparring with one another to lead the herd.

The mouth consisted of a big beak, teeth that could chop up tough plants, and cheek pouches to hold the food while it was chewed.

66 MYA

CAMBRIAN	ORDOVICIAN	SILURIAN	DEVONIAN	CARBONIFEROUS	PERMIAN	TRIASSIC	JURASSIC	CRETACEOUS	CENOZOIC

Name: *Triceratops* (try–SEH–ra–tops)
Sub–order: Ceratopsia
Length: 9 m (30 ft)
Weight: 9 tonnes (9.9 tons)

ANIMAL PROFILE

DID YOU KNOW? When the fossil horns were first discovered, they were thought to have come from giant bison.

Ankylosaurus

With so many huge carnivorous dinosaurs around at the end of the Cretaceous period, many of the plant-eaters developed coverings of shields and masses of heavy plates and scales. These shields, plates, and scales worked like protective chain mail. The thyreophorans, relatives of Jurassic *Stegosaurus*, became the most heavily defended of all.

Living Tank

Ankylosaurus was the most heavily protected of all the thyreophorans. Its head and back were covered with strong bony knobs, and it had a massive club at the end of its tail. Even its eyelids were like steel shutters, slamming down whenever danger approached. The biggest meat-eaters of the time would have found it difficult to penetrate these barriers.

Some scientists think that the club had eye spots to make it look like a head and confuse an attacker.

The tail club was made of solid bone, and the tail bones were fused together so that it could be swung around like a mace.

CAMBRIAN	ORDOVICIAN	SILURIAN	DEVONIAN	CARBONIFEROUS	PERMIAN	TRIASSIC	JURASSIC	CRETACEOUS	CENOZOIC

66 MYA

Name: *Ankylosaurus*
(an-KIH-loh-SORE-us)
Clade: Thyreophora
Length: 8 m (26 ft)
Weight: 8 tonnes (8.8 tons)

ANIMAL PROFILE

An arrangement of large bony plates called osteoderms were set into the skin in regular rows to protect the back.

Club or Spike?

There were two main types of thyreophorans at the end of the Cretaceous: the ankylosaurs, which had a club at the end of the tail, and the nodosaurs, which had no tail club but defended themselves with huge spikes on their shoulders.

Sauropelta was a typical nodosaur with shoulder spines. At 6 m (20 ft) long, it was one of the biggest of the group.

The underside was protected by a tight pattern of smaller scales. There were osteoderms protecting the upper arm.

DID YOU KNOW? We have never found a complete skeleton of *Ankylosaurus*, but we can tell what it looked like by looking at its more complete relatives.

Mosasaurus

The really big hunters in the oceans at the very end of the Cretaceous period were the mosasaurs. They belonged to the squamate group—the same group that contains today's lizards and snakes. Their closest living relatives are the monitor lizards, such as the komodo dragon.

Sea Lizard

To imagine *Mosasaurus,* picture a giant monitor lizard, but with a fluke (whale's tail) on the end of its tail, and its legs and feet converted into paddles. Now picture it as big as a whale. This is what *Mosasaurus* looked like! With its tail, paddles, and streamlined shape, it had the same adaptations for a swimming lifestyle as the earlier ichthyosaurs (see page 28).

The jaws of *Mosasaurus* were long, narrow, and armed with sharp fish-catching teeth.

The toes were fused together to form a swimming paddle.

Mosasaurus and most other mosasaurs had sharp teeth for fish-catching, but some had blunt, rounded teeth for cracking shellfish.

DID YOU KNOW? Mosasaurs appeared when the ichthyosaurs died out.

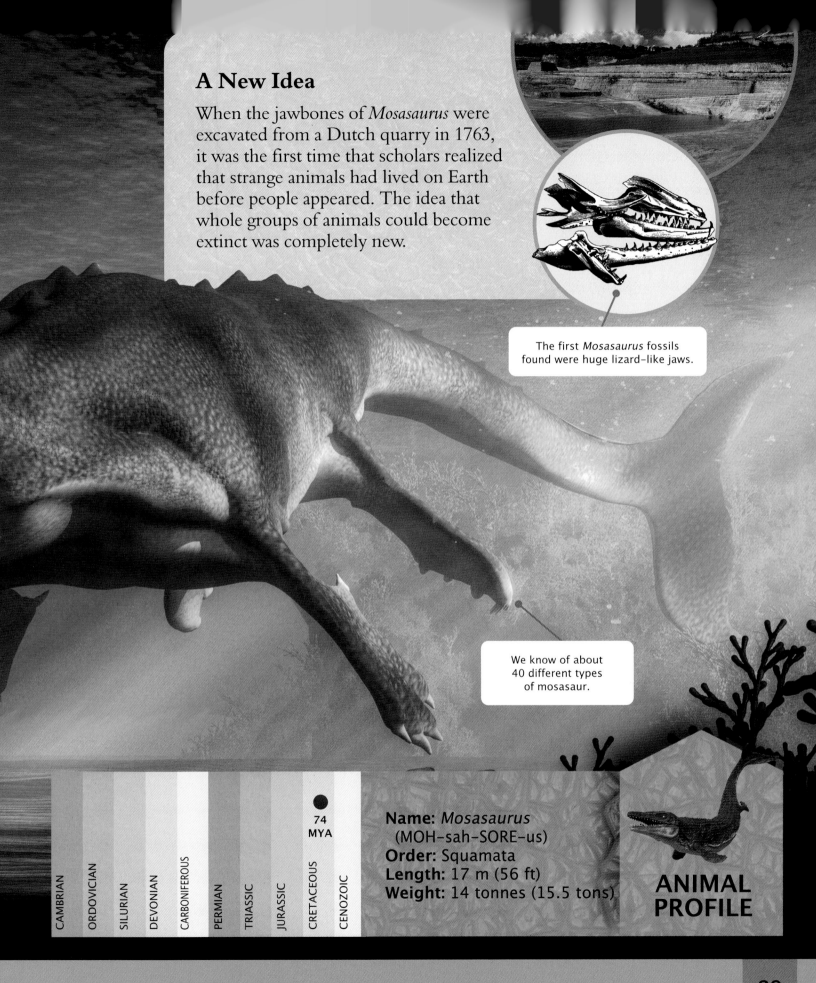

A New Idea

When the jawbones of *Mosasaurus* were excavated from a Dutch quarry in 1763, it was the first time that scholars realized that strange animals had lived on Earth before people appeared. The idea that whole groups of animals could become extinct was completely new.

The first *Mosasaurus* fossils found were huge lizard–like jaws.

We know of about 40 different types of mosasaur.

74 MYA

CAMBRIAN

ORDOVICIAN

SILURIAN

DEVONIAN

CARBONIFEROUS

PERMIAN

TRIASSIC

JURASSIC

CRETACEOUS

CENOZOIC

Name: *Mosasaurus*
(MOH–sah–SORE–us)
Order: Squamata
Length: 17 m (56 ft)
Weight: 14 tonnes (15.5 tons)

ANIMAL PROFILE

Deinosuchus

It is often said that crocodiles have remained unchanged since the days of the dinosaurs. This is broadly true, and there were some prehistoric crocodiles very much like today's cold-blooded ambush hunters. But the crocodiles of today are much smaller. In the Cretaceous period, some of them were huge!

Terror of the Swamp

Deinosuchus was a giant crocodile that lived in North America. It looked somewhat like a modern crocodile, but was very much bigger. It preferred brackish water (a mix of fresh and salt water) and lived in coastal swamps and river mouths. It hunted turtles and any big animal that came to the river to drink.

Sarcosuchus, a relative of *Deinosuchus*, was the terror of the African dinosaurs, on the other side of the new Atlantic Ocean.

The broad snout of *Deinosuchus* helped it seize unsuspecting prey and pull it into the water.

CAMBRIAN	ORDOVICIAN	SILURIAN	DEVONIAN	CARBONIFEROUS	PERMIAN	TRIASSIC	JURASSIC	CRETACEOUS	CENOZOIC

75 MYA

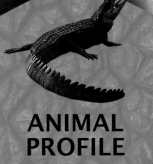

Name: *Deinosuchus* (dy-no-SOO-kus)
Order: Crocodylia
Length: 11 m (35 ft)
Weight: 4 tonnes (4.4 tons)

ANIMAL PROFILE

While the big theropods such as *Gorgosaurus* were the main hunters on dry land, the big crocodiles like *Deinosuchus* were the main hunters in the rivers.

A Crocodilian Variety

Other crocodiles existed at the time, including elegant running crocodiles, fish-eating crocodiles, and even vegetarian crocodiles. However, only the water-dwelling ambush hunting crocodiles have survived until today.

Kaprosuchus was a land-living hunting crocodile. Because of its huge tusks, it has been nicknamed the "boar croc."

Like a modern crocodile, *Deinosuchus* lurked just below water level before leaping out on is prey.

DID YOU KNOW? *Deinosuchus* continued to grow for most of its 50-year life span. It just got bigger and bigger!

Dolichorhynchops

Back in Jurassic times, the swimming plesiosaurs were divided into two groups—the long-necked plesiosauroids and the big-headed pliosauroids (see page 46). By the end of the Cretaceous, the plesiosauroids were still flourishing, but the pliosauroids were all gone. A new group of long-headed plesiosaurs developed from the plesiosauroid line to fill their place.

A New Shape

Dolichorhynchops was the new long-headed plesiosaur. It combined the long jaws of the pliosauroids with the flexible neck of the plesiosauroids. It was a medium-sized animal and seems to have hunted in deeper waters than its relatives. Like a modern whale, it needed to come to the surface to breathe. Its rivals were the big swimming lizards, the mosasaurs (see page 90).

Dolichorhynchops was hunted by the big mosasaurs of the time. Bones of one have been found in the skeleton of the mosasaur *Tylosaurus*.

Dolichorhynchops gave birth to live young, so it did not need to come ashore to lay eggs.

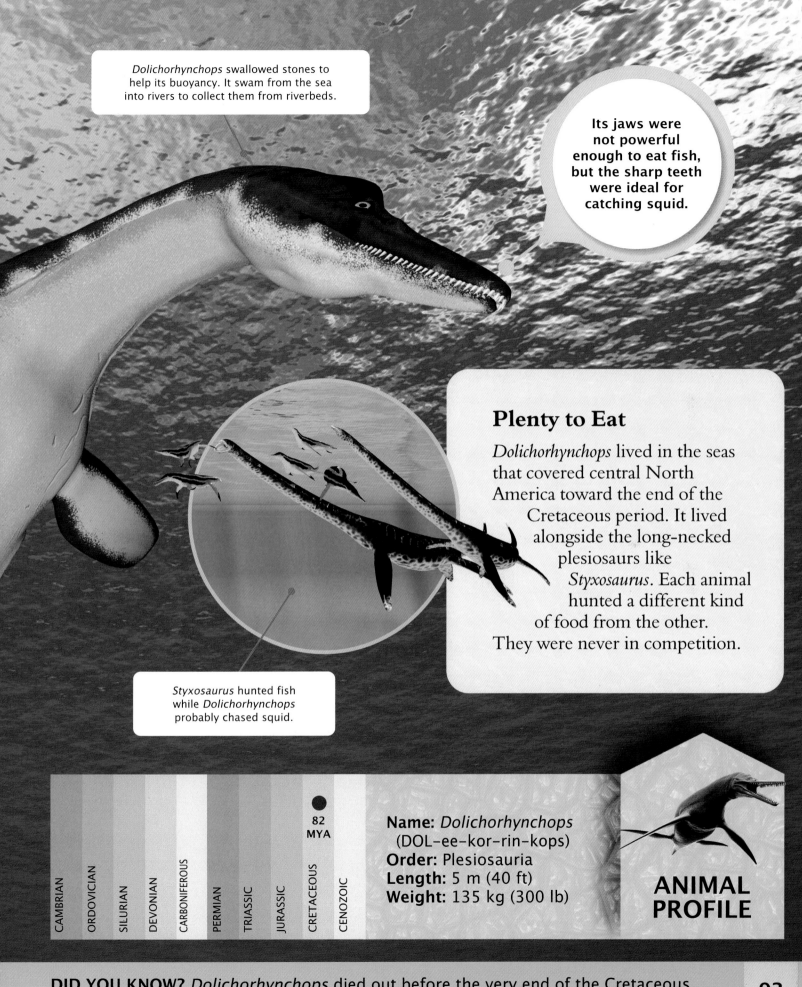

Dolichorhynchops swallowed stones to help its buoyancy. It swam from the sea into rivers to collect them from riverbeds.

Its jaws were not powerful enough to eat fish, but the sharp teeth were ideal for catching squid.

Plenty to Eat

Dolichorhynchops lived in the seas that covered central North America toward the end of the Cretaceous period. It lived alongside the long-necked plesiosaurs like *Styxosaurus*. Each animal hunted a different kind of food from the other. They were never in competition.

Styxosaurus hunted fish while *Dolichorhynchops* probably chased squid.

82 MYA

CAMBRIAN ORDOVICIAN SILURIAN DEVONIAN CARBONIFEROUS PERMIAN TRIASSIC JURASSIC CRETACEOUS CENOZOIC

Name: *Dolichorhynchops* (DOL-ee-kor-rin-kops)
Order: Plesiosauria
Length: 5 m (40 ft)
Weight: 135 kg (300 lb)

ANIMAL PROFILE

DID YOU KNOW? *Dolichorhynchops* died out before the very end of the Cretaceous.

Alphadon

The mammals had appeared at about the same time as the dinosaurs, back in late Triassic times. However, they spent the Cretaceous—the age of dinosaurs—as small, insignificant creatures. Despite that, there were many different types, ready to take over once the great dinosaurs were gone.

Delicate Fossils

The early mammals were so small that we don't often find fossils of them. We know about most of them from fossils of their teeth. Teeth are much harder than bones and can fossilize more easily. We can compare the fossil teeth with the teeth of modern mammals and figure out what kind of animal they belonged to. From its teeth, we can tell that *Alphadon* was like a modern opossum.

The mammals of Cretaceous times hid themselves in the undergrowth, burrows, trees, and beneath the foliage of the new flowering plants.

In the second half of the Cretaceous period, there were many new forms of mammals appearing, just as there were many new forms of dinosaurs. This is probably because different plants were appearing at the time, producing new types of food.

Speed and agility helped warm-blooded *Alphadon* escape the bigger meat-eating dinosaurs such as *Stenonychosaurus*.

Purgatorius belonged to a group that did survive. It may have been the ancestor of primates, including ourselves.

Many Types

The mammals flourished in the undergrowth at the feet of the dinosaurs. In Cretaceous times, they developed into almost all the shapes and lifestyles that we would associate with small mammals today. However, having the same shapes does not mean that they were closely related to today's small mammals. They almost all belonged to groups that have since become extinct. Only a few survived and gave rise to today's mammal life.

Dinosaurs certainly ruled the world at the end of the Cretaceous period, but they were soon to be replaced by the mammals.

75 MYA

CAMBRIAN | ORDOVICIAN | SILURIAN | DEVONIAN | CARBONIFEROUS | PERMIAN | TRIASSIC | JURASSIC | CRETACEOUS | CENOZOIC

Name: *Alphadon*
(AL-fa-don)
Class: Mammalia
Length: 30 cm (12 in)
Weight: 1.5 kg (3.3 lb)

ANIMAL PROFILE

DID YOU KNOW? *Alphadon* may have been a marsupial, meaning that it would have carried its youngsters in a pouch.

Chapter 5

All change

Suddenly, they were all gone! All the giant reptiles—the flying and swimming reptiles, the long-necked plant-eating dinosaurs, the horned and shielded types, the terrifying carnivores—were all gone. All the big animals were wiped out by a terrible disaster. A meteorite as big as a small town crashed into Earth, bringing the Cretaceous period to an end with worldwide devastation.

A New Beginning

It was the small animals that survived and took over. During the Age of Reptiles, the little mammals were small and insignificant. Now they were able to spread out and take over the world. They grew into all the niches that the dinosaurs and the other big reptiles had occupied. From little mouse-like creatures, they became big plant-eaters, fierce hunters, swimmers, and fliers. The Cenozoic era—the Age of Mammals—had begun.

Mammals even took to the air. *Icaronycterys* was one of the first bats.

A Family of Survivors

Kimbetopsalis evolved from a group of small mammals, called multituberculates, that survived the meteorite disaster. Once plants began to flourish after the meteorite strike and fresh environments opened up, multituberculates could adapt to new niches that were now available. *Kimbetopsalis* was ideal for adaptation: its shape was not specialized and it could eat almost any food.

The tail was long and heavy. It acted like a tightrope-walker's pole, keeping *Darwinius* steady while it walked on branches.

A basic mammal shape—body, tail, four legs, and a head—was the perfect starting point to develop into all kinds of other shapes.

DID YOU KNOW? *Darwinius* is named after Charles Darwin, the nineteenth-century biologist who was the first to realize how evolution worked.

Megacerops

Soon after the mammals took over from the dinosaurs, they developed a few basic shapes that seemed to work for particular lifestyles. One of those shapes was the heavy plant-eater with horns on its head. We can still see that shape today as the rhinoceros.

Rhino Look-Alike

Hoofed mammals come in two families: the Perissodactyla, with an odd number of toes, and the Artiodactyla, with an even number of toes. The perissodactyls include the rhinos, the horses, and other groups that are now extinct. *Megacerops* was an elephant-sized perissodactyl that looked like a rhinoceros, but it was more closely related to horses.

The horns of *Megacerops* were bony structures covered in skin, like those of a modern giraffe.

Arsinoitherium was an early two-horned rhinoceros shape from Africa. It had the same body shape but was not actually related to the perissodactyls.

35 MYA

Name: *Megacerops*
(MEG-ah-sehr-ops)
Order: Perissodactyla
Length: 4.6 m (15 ft)
Weight: 3.8 tonnes (4.2 tons)

CAMBRIAN	ORDOVICIAN	SILURIAN	DEVONIAN	CARBONIFEROUS	PERMIAN	TRIASSIC	JURASSIC	CRETACEOUS	CENOZOIC

ANIMAL PROFILE

DID YOU KNOW? *Megacerops* used to be known as *Brontotherium*—the thunder beast.

The Real Rhinos

The true rhinoceroses appeared at about the same time as *Megacerops* and developed into strange shapes. *Paraceratherium* was one of the tallest land animals that ever lived—about 7.4 m (34 ft) high. In comparison, the tallest modern giraffe is about 5.5 m (18 ft) high. Although it was a true rhinoceros, *Paraceratherium* did not have a horn on its nose.

Herds of *Paraceratherium* roamed the plains of Central Asia 30 million years ago.

Fossils of *Megacerops* have been found with broken ribs. They must have used their horned heads to fight one another.

Daeodon

These days, the artiodactyls—the even-toed ungulates—are gentle, plant-eating beasts. They include animals such as sheep, camels, and giraffes. But back in the Age of Mammals, there were some truly ferocious meat-eating types.

Carnivorous Pig

Daeodon is sometimes referred to as the "hell pig." It looked something like a wild boar, but it was taller than you are at its shoulders. It had long muscular legs built for running and chasing down swift-footed prey. Not many fossils have been found, suggesting that *Daeodon* was a solitary animal that hunted alone.

Another meat–eating artiodactyl was *Andrewsarchus*, which was like a gigantic wolf. Earlier than *Daeodon*, it prowled the forests in the Age of Mammals.

That's More Like It

The plant-eating artiodactyls were around at that time, too. They had evolved to live on the new environments of grassy plains. The ancestors of the camels and giraffes grazed the open landscape—and often fell prey to fierce hunters like *Daeodon*.

The later *Sivatherium* was a kind of early giraffe, but looked more like a moose.

Like other artiodactyls, *Daeodon* had two hooves on each foot.

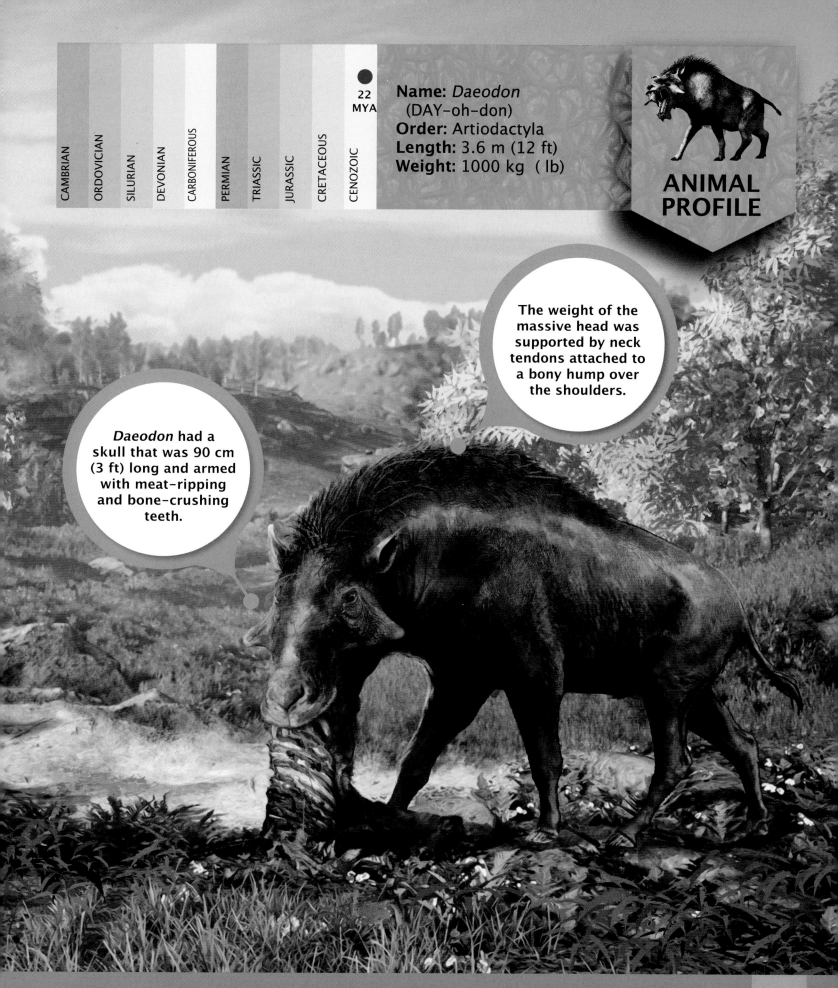

● 22 MYA

Name: *Daeodon* (DAY–oh–don)
Order: Artiodactyla
Length: 3.6 m (12 ft)
Weight: 1000 kg (lb)

ANIMAL PROFILE

The weight of the massive head was supported by neck tendons attached to a bony hump over the shoulders.

Daeodon had a skull that was 90 cm (3 ft) long and armed with meat-ripping and bone-crushing teeth.

DID YOU KNOW? Despite its ferocity, *Daeodon* was omnivorous. It ate plants as well as meat.

Deinotherium

We all know what an elephant looks like. It's the biggest land animal we have today, thick skinned, with a pair of tusks and a flexible trunk. Elephants have been around since the beginning of the Age of Mammals, but the earliest were pig-sized creatures. They developed into a number of strange forms throughout their history.

Deinotherium was built like an African elephant, but its legs were longer. It could run faster over open plains.

A Giant Elephant

The biggest and best known of the ancient elephants was *Deinotherium*. It was built like a modern elephant but was much bigger. Unlike today's elephants, its tusks were on the lower jaw and curved downward. *Deinotherium* existed for several million years, first appearing in Africa. Then it spread to Europe and India. It did not die out until the Ice Age.

Moeritherium was one of the first of the elephants. It was about the size of a pig and lived partly in the water, like a hippopotamus.

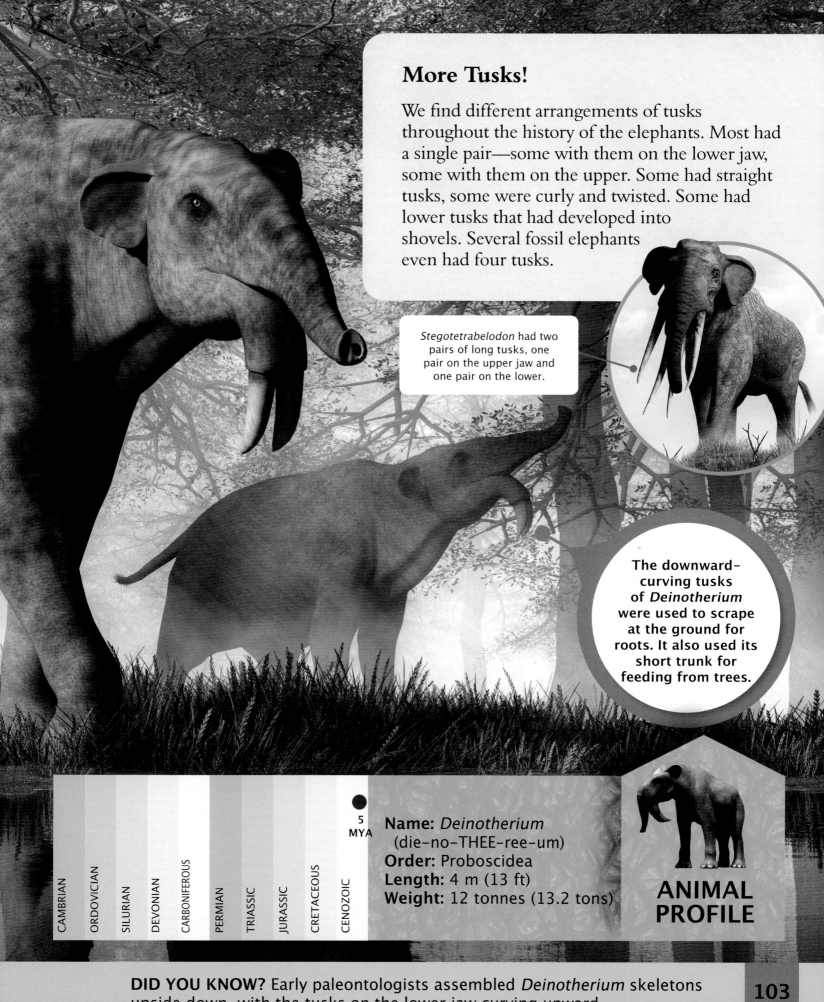

More Tusks!

We find different arrangements of tusks throughout the history of the elephants. Most had a single pair—some with them on the lower jaw, some with them on the upper. Some had straight tusks, some were curly and twisted. Some had lower tusks that had developed into shovels. Several fossil elephants even had four tusks.

Stegotetrabelodon had two pairs of long tusks, one pair on the upper jaw and one pair on the lower.

The downward-curving tusks of *Deinotherium* were used to scrape at the ground for roots. It also used its short trunk for feeding from trees.

CAMBRIAN ORDOVICIAN SILURIAN DEVONIAN CARBONIFEROUS PERMIAN TRIASSIC JURASSIC CRETACEOUS CENOZOIC

5 MYA

Name: *Deinotherium*
(die–no–THEE–ree–um)
Order: Proboscidea
Length: 4 m (13 ft)
Weight: 12 tonnes (13.2 tons)

ANIMAL PROFILE

DID YOU KNOW? Early paleontologists assembled *Deinotherium* skeletons upside down, with the tusks on the lower jaw curving upward.

Basilosaurus

As the mammals expanded into all environments, they took to the sea as well. They took over the roles once occupied by ichthyosaurs, plesiosaurs, and mosasaurs. They became totally adapted to a seagoing life, and they live on today as the whales.

Basilosaurus moved through the ocean with an undulating, up-and-down motion, driven by its tail and steered by its forelimbs.

Life as a Swimmer

Like the marine reptiles in earlier times, the body of a completely aquatic mammal needs to be streamlined so it can slide through the water easily. The limbs and tail are turned into fins and paddles for locomotion. We can see this in the early whale *Basilosaurus*, which looked something like a sea serpent.

The teeth of *Basilosaurus* were perfect for catching other early whales and big sharks.

40 MYA

CAMBRIAN	ORDOVICIAN	SILURIAN	DEVONIAN	CARBONIFEROUS	PERMIAN	TRIASSIC	JURASSIC	CRETACEOUS	CENOZOIC

Name: *Basilosaurus* (bas-il-oh-SAWR-us)
Infraorder: Cetacea
Length: 18 m (59 ft)
Weight: 6.5 tonnes (7.2 tons)

ANIMAL PROFILE

The very long backbone of *Basilosaurus* consisted of more than 70 vertebrae.

Like modern whales, *Basilosaurus* lost the use of is hind legs, and they eventually almost disappeared.

A Gradual Progression

We can trace the development of the whale shape over several millions of years—from a totally land-living animal, through various amphibious stages, to the complete marine animal that we would recognize today. At first, they took to the water only sometimes and lived like otters or hippos. Gradually, they spent more time there and developed more fishlike shapes.

When in the water, *Ambulocetus* could swim using its broad feet and its tail.

Ambulocetus was as big as a sea lion and spent much of its time on land.

DID YOU KNOW? *Basilosaurus* sounds more like a dinosaur than a whale. Its first discoverer thought he had found a giant reptile and gave it a name meaning "emperor lizard."

Kelenken

The shape of the big, ferocious theropod dinosaurs was so effective that it appeared again in the Age of Mammals. A group of ground-living, meat-eating birds called the phorusrhacids looked like the now-extinct dinosaurs, with their strong hind legs, tiny arms, and big heads. Unlike dinosaurs, they did not have large tails, but they were just as fierce.

Another large bird, *Gastornis*, lived earlier in North America, Europe, and China.

The Top Predator

Kelenken is the biggest phorusrhachid known. It had strong running legs and could chase down smaller, swift mammals on the open pampas plains. It could swallow small animals whole and kill bigger animals with its strong break. It was probably a scavenger too, eating anything it found which was already dead (carrion).

Unlike the meat-eating dinosaurs, the phorusrhacids did not have a long tail.

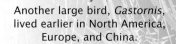

CAMBRIAN	ORDOVICIAN	SILURIAN	DEVONIAN	CARBONIFEROUS	PERMIAN	TRIASSIC	JURASSIC	CRETACEOUS	CENOZOIC

15 MYA

Name: *Kelenken*
(kel–ehn–ken)
Order: Cariamiformes
Height: 3 m (10 ft)
Weight: 100 kg (220 lb)

ANIMAL PROFILE

DID YOU KNOW? The name *Keleken* comes from the name of a spirit in stories told by people in the part of Argentina where the fossil was found.

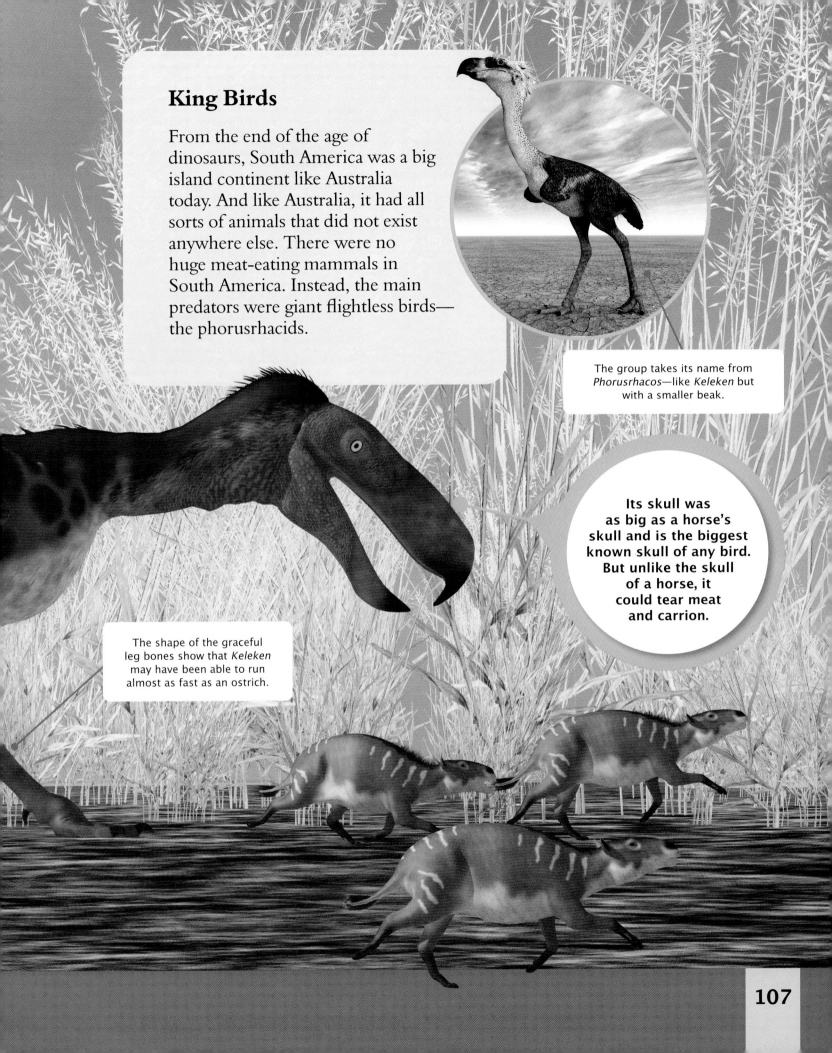

King Birds

From the end of the age of dinosaurs, South America was a big island continent like Australia today. And like Australia, it had all sorts of animals that did not exist anywhere else. There were no huge meat-eating mammals in South America. Instead, the main predators were giant flightless birds—the phorusrhacids.

The group takes its name from *Phorusrhacos*—like *Keleken* but with a smaller beak.

Its skull was as big as a horse's skull and is the biggest known skull of any bird. But unlike the skull of a horse, it could tear meat and carrion.

The shape of the graceful leg bones show that *Keleken* may have been able to run almost as fast as an ostrich.

Megalodon

The biggest hunter in the sea during the Age of Mammals was a gigantic shark. Its scientific name is *Otodus megalodon*, but it is usually just called megalodon, meaning "giant tooth". It hunted in all the tropical oceans of our planet until it died out at the beginning of the Ice Age.

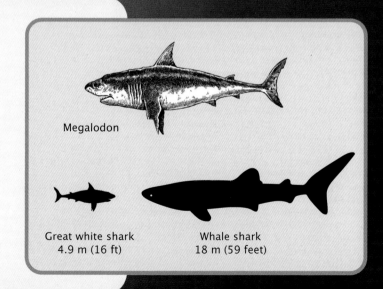

Megalodon hunted whales, dolphins, and sharks in tropical oceans around the world.

Ruler of the Oceans

Megalodon existed in the oceans for about 20 million years in the later Age of Mammals. It probably died out when the oceans cooled and the Ice Age began to get underway. Its numbers declined at the same time as the biggest whales appeared. The whales may have competed with megalodon for food.

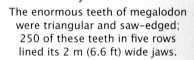

The enormous teeth of megalodon were triangular and saw-edged; 250 of these teeth in five rows lined its 2 m (6.6 ft) wide jaws.

Dental Record

Almost everything we know of this massive animal comes from fossils of its teeth. The rest of the skeleton was made of cartilage rather than bone, and cartilage does not fossilize easily. So we are not sure about its appearance or its full size. If it looked like a modern great white shark, it may have been 16 m (52 ft) long. If it looked more like a modern whale shark, it could have been 20 m (67 ft) long.

Megalodon

Great white shark
4.9 m (16 ft)

Whale shark
18 m (59 feet)

Some rare fossils of megalodon backbones show annual growth rings. These tell us that megalodon could live for about 40 years.

The gigantic sperm whale *Livyatan* was big enough to hunt and eat megalodon itself.

CAMBRIAN	ORDOVICIAN	SILURIAN	DEVONIAN	CARBONIFEROUS	PERMIAN	TRIASSIC	JURASSIC	CRETACEOUS	CENOZOIC

10 MYA

Name: *Otodus megalodon*
(ot-oh-dus me-GA-lo-don)
Class: Chondrichthyes
Length: 16 m (52 ft)
Weight: 61 tonnes (68 tons)

ANIMAL PROFILE

DID YOU KNOW? Modern sharks give birth in nursery areas. Fossil megalodon nursery areas have been found in Central America and Spain.

Chapter 6

Ice Age

The Pleistocene Ice Age gripped the world for two million years, especially the continents in the northern hemisphere. Glaciers spread and retreated time and time again. During those frozen times, many animals adapted to the cold conditions by becoming larger and growing hairy coats. The woolly mammoth is the most familiar of these.

Elephant of the Cold

There were a few different species of mammoth—some big, some small, some with thick hair, some with very little hair, some that fed on grass, and some that fed on leaves. The woolly mammoth is the one we know most about. It did not die out until about 4,000 years ago. Its closest living relative is the Indian elephant.

A fatty hump on the mammoth's back stored energy for when the conditions were particularly harsh and there was no food available.

Our early ancestors hunted and ate woolly mammoths. They also painted them on cave walls.

CAMBRIAN
ORDOVICIAN
SILURIAN
DEVONIAN
CARBONIFEROUS
PERMIAN
TRIASSIC
JURASSIC
CRETACEOUS
CENOZOIC

0.2 MYA

Name: *Mammuthus primigenius* (MAM-uth-us PRY-mi-jee-nee-us)
Order: Proboscidea
Length: 3 m (10 ft)
Weight: 6 tonnes (6.6 tons)

ANIMAL PROFILE

DID YOU KNOW? A mammoth's hair could be black, reddish-brown, or red. It varied between individuals.

The ears of the mammoth were small to reduce heat loss and prevent frostbite in the cold.

Frozen Remains

We have found many frozen mammoth bodies buried in the frosted soils of northern America and Asia. These mammoths were caught and drowned in frozen bogs. Their flesh was preserved as if they were in a freezer.

Some of the frozen mammoths' flesh was still fresh enough to be eaten by the dogs of the expeditions that found them.

Footprints show that mammoths lived in herds. The herds consisted of adults and youngsters. Each herd was led by a big female.

Woolly Rhinoceros

Its body was deep to hold a big digestive system, so that it could get the best nutrition out of the tough, poor quality food that it ate.

The cold conditions of the Ice Age produced chilly grasslands and icy, boggy tundra landscapes across the northern continents. The woolly rhinoceros was one of the animals that developed to deal with the cold conditions.

Rhino portraits

Like the woolly mammoth (see page 110), we know what woolly rhinoceroses looked like because we have found their preserved in frozen mud, and also because our ancestors painted pictures of them on cave walls. The woolly rhinoceros had a hump on its shoulder, a long horn, and was covered in shaggy hair.

Elasmotherium was another Ice Age rhinoceros with a massive horn on its head.

The nose bones were thicker and stronger than those of a modern rhinoceros to support the weight of the horn.

Humpback

The skeleton of the woolly rhinoceros shows high spines over its shoulders. These would have held strong neck muscles to support the enormous weight of the head and the horn. They might also have held a store of fat, like the hump of the woolly mammoth or the modern camel, to nourish the animal when food was scarce.

● 0.2 MYA

Name: *Coelodonta*
(SEE–low–DON–ta)
Order: Perissodactyla
Length: 3.6 m (11.8 ft)
Weight: 2 tonnes (2.2 tons)

ANIMAL PROFILE

The horn, like that of a modern rhinoceros, was made of compacted hair. Unlike the horns of goats and antelopes today, it did not have a core of bone.

The woolly rhinoceros lived on open plains, where it ate grasses and low-growing plants. It used its cropping front teeth and broad muscular lips to gather food.

DID YOU KNOW? The woolly rhinoceros died out when climate change at the end of the Ice Age reduced the tough grass that it liked to eat.

Titanis

The flightless terror birds, the phorusrhacids (see page 106), evolved in South America. Later, they moved into North America when a land bridge joined the two continents. *Titanis* was the most notable of the terror birds. However, the phorusrhacids were not the only big flightless birds of the Ice Age.

We have never found a fossil of the beak of *Titanis*, but we can compare the rest of the animal with other phorusrhacids and see that it must have been a big killing weapon.

Feathered Hunter

There were terror birds in North America before *Titanis* arrived, but they had already been extinct for millions of years when it migrated northward. Once in North America, *Titanis* was a very successful hunter, rivalling fierce mammals such as the big cats, large dogs, and bears that were already there.

Aepyornis was a 3 m (10 ft) tall "elephant bird" not closely related to *Titanis*. It was a big ground dwelling bird of Madagascar that became extinct about 700 years ago.

Another group of flightless birds was *Dinornis*, also called the moa. It was 3.6 m (12 ft) tall and lived in New Zealand until about 600 years ago. It was taller but lighter than *Aepyornis* and not as fierce as *Titanis*.

CAMBRIAN	ORDOVICIAN	SILURIAN	DEVONIAN	CARBONIFEROUS	PERMIAN	TRIASSIC	JURASSIC	CRETACEOUS	CENOZOIC

2 MYA

Name: *Titanis*
(ty–TAN–is)
Order: Cariamiformes
Height: 1.9 m (6.2 ft)
Weight: 150 kg (330 lb)

ANIMAL PROFILE

DID YOU KNOW? *Titanis* was the first creature that we know of to cross the Central American land bridge and move north.

The muscles in the neck of *Titanis* gave the killer beak a hammer-like impact.

Isolation

Most large ground-living birds in recent times lived on islands. This is because new islands don't usually have big, fierce hunters on them, so the birds don't need to fly away from danger. They can take up a ground-living existence. Sometimes they even become the big, fierce hunters themselves.

The dodo of Mauritius was an island-living flightless bird. It was wiped out in the seventeenth century when explorers arrived, bringing rats and dogs with them.

Glossotherium

The giant ground sloths, the mylodonts, were herbivorous mammals that flourished in South America in Cretaceous and Cenozoic times. Later, new volcanic land rose out of the sea and linked South and North America, making a land bridge for them to migrate northward.

Paramylodon, a close relative of *Glossotherium*, also migrated north into North America. Its remains have been found in tar pits in Los Angeles.

A Burrowing Giant

Glossotherium was one of the giant ground sloths, although it was small compared to many of the others. It lived and fed on the grassy plains, or Pampas, of South America. It may have sheltered in tunnels that it dug into the hard Pampas soils. These tunnels were up to 1.8 m (6 ft) in diameter and tens of meters long. Scratch marks on the walls match the huge claws on the hands of *Glossotherium*.

Glossotherium was so big that it had few enemies. The sabertoothed *Smilodon* (see page 120) migrated southward from North America and preyed on the ground sloths.

Big Body, Poor Food

Grass is not very nutritious. Animals that eat it need very complex digestive systems—for example, cows have four stomachs and need to chew their food several times (see *Aurochs*, page 122). The gut of *Glossotherium* was a big fermentation vat for processing grass. The animal lived at a slow, almost cold-blooded rate, so that it did not need much energy.

The great barrel-shaped body of *Glossotherium* contained a huge digestive system.

Glossotherium did not chew its food. Its teeth grew constantly and were suited for shearing the leaves from shrubs.

The spade-like front feet of Glossotherium were good for digging in the ground. This giant sloth was the biggest burrowing animal ever.

0.3 MYA

Name: *Glossotherium*
(GLOSS–oh–the–ree–um)
Family: Mylodontidae
Length: 4 m (13 ft)
Weight: 1.5 tonnes
(1.6 tons)

CAMBRIAN | ORDOVICIAN | SILURIAN | DEVONIAN | CARBONIFEROUS | PERMIAN | TRIASSIC | JURASSIC | CRETACEOUS | CENOZOIC

ANIMAL PROFILE

DID YOU KNOW? *Glossotherium* communicated in low-frequency grunts. These noises carried well on open plains, which is why modern elephants use them.

117

Doedicurus

The modern armadillo is an unusual little animal, protected by a complete articulated shield. It is found in both North and South America, but it originated on the southern continent. Some of its Ice Age relatives there were truly enormous.

A Living Fortress

The glyptodonts were the huge armadillos of South America. There were several different types. They roamed across the South American Pampas, feeding on the tough grasses that grew there. *Doedicurus* was the biggest of them—the size of a modern family car.

The shell of a glyptodont was a solid dome, not like the articulated covering of a modern armadillo.

A modern armadillo hunts and eats insects, unlike its Ice Age vegetarian relatives.

CAMBRIAN	ORDOVICIAN	SILURIAN	DEVONIAN	CARBONIFEROUS	PERMIAN	TRIASSIC	JURASSIC	CRETACEOUS	CENOZOIC

1 MYA

Name: *Doedicurus*
(doh–DIK–ur–us)
Sub–family: Glyptodontinae
Length: 3.6 m (14.5 ft)
Weight: 1.4 tonnes
(1.5 tons)

ANIMAL PROFILE

The tail club of *Ankylosaurus*, like that of *Doedicurus*, was made of bones fused together.

Tail for Protection

The club at the end of *Doedicurus'* tail was nothing new. The dinosaur *Ankylosaurus* (see page 88) had a similar weapon. The tail's stiff shaft, flexible at the base, meant that the club could be swung with force against an attacker. The two animals were not related. The fact that they developed an identical weapon is what scientists call "convergence."

Spikes on the tail club gave it the appearance of a medieval mace.

Doedicurus was balanced at the hips. This means that it might have raised itself on its hind legs to feed from trees.

DID YOU KNOW? *Doedicurus* was the last surviving glyptodont. It may have still been around on the South American plains, 7,000 years ago.

Smilodon

The fiercest predators that fed on the big mammals of the later Cenozoic era were the sabertooth cats. Feel the pair of pointed teeth that you have at each side of the front of your mouth. These are your canines. Those teeth grew into huge blade-like weapons in the Ice Age predators.

Smilodon's mouth could open wider than that of any other cats. When it was closed, the saber teeth lay at each side of the lower jaw.

The Biggest and the Fiercest

Bigger than a modern tiger, *Smilodon* was the biggest of the sabertooth cats. It ambushed its prey, leaping out of cover on its strong rear feet, bringing its victim down with its powerful front legs, and using the long saber teeth to inflict killing wounds.

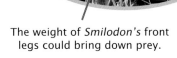

The weight of *Smilodon*'s front legs could bring down prey.

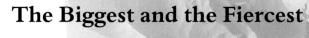

1 MYA

Name: *Smilodon*
(SMY–lo–don)
Family: Felidae
Length: 2.3 m (8 ft)
Weight: 436 kg (960 lb)

ANIMAL PROFILE

CAMBRIAN	ORDOVICIAN	SILURIAN	DEVONIAN	CARBONIFEROUS	PERMIAN	TRIASSIC	JURASSIC	CRETACEOUS	CENOZOIC

DID YOU KNOW? The best *Smilodon* fossils have been found in tar pits in the middle of Los Angeles, California.

Deadly Weapons

Look at how the curve of the skull continues down into the curve of the saber teeth. When the teeth were brought down in a killing action, they had the full force of the muscular neck behind them—like a hammer swung down from the shoulders.

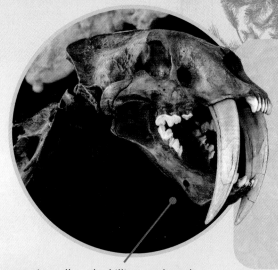

As well as the killing teeth at the front of its mouth, *Smilodon* had meat-shearing teeth at the back.

Hunting cats with long tails use them for balance and steering while running. *Smilodon*'s short tail shows that it was an ambusher rather than a chaser.

We do not know what kind of coat *Smilodon* had or whether it had a lion's mane.

Aurochs

The aurochs was a kind of gigantic cattle of the Pleistocene Ice Age that existed up until historical times. It first appeared in eastern Asia, and moved to India and Africa during periods when the ice retreated for a while. It ended up in Northern Europe in modern times.

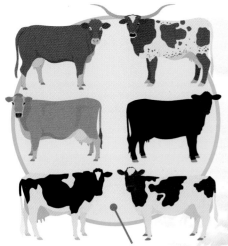

Modern cows have many varieties, but we don't know if aurochs coats varied.

A Grass-Processing Machine

Aurochs and other wild cattle can digest grass that other animals cannot. It possessed four stomachs to help digestion, and now and then the food was passed back to its mouth for another chew—"chewing the cud." This ability allowed the aurochs to flourish on the grasslands of Ice Age Europe and Asia. But the wild form of cattle became extinct as the climate changed and human agriculture spread across the grasslands.

The Great Beast Tamed

The aurochs is the ancestor of all our domestic cattle. From it were bred all the varieties that we have used throughout our history, as well as the familiar forms— elegant milking cows and massive beef cattle—that we know today. The fierceness of the aurochs has been bred out of them as well, making them less dangerous.

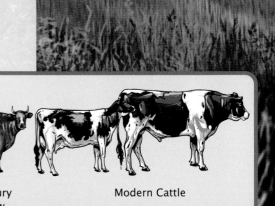

Our ancestors recognized how efficient the wild cattle were and began to domesticate them about 8,000 years ago.

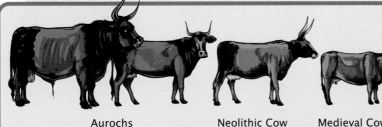

| Aurochs | Neolithic Cow | Medieval Cow | 17th–Century Dutch Cow | Modern Cattle |

There have been a number of attempts to resurrect the aurochs by breeding from modern varieties. So far, this has not been successful.

A male aurochs stood 180 cm (6 ft) at the shoulders. Its huge horns were 80 cm (30 in) long. Its image was painted on cave walls by paleolithic humans.

CAMBRIAN
ORDOVICIAN
SILURIAN
DEVONIAN
CARBONIFEROUS
PERMIAN
TRIASSIC
JURASSIC
CRETACEOUS
CENOZOIC

1 MYA

Name: *Bos primigenius* (boss PRY-mi-jee-nee-us)
Order: Artiodactyla
Length: 3 m (10 ft)
Weight: 1,500 kg (3,310 lb)

ANIMAL PROFILE

DID YOU KNOW? The last aurochs died in Poland in 1627.

Irish Elk

We call *Megaloceros* the "Irish elk" because the best remains have been found in peat bogs in Ireland. But it ranged from Ireland all across the north of Europe and Asia to Lake Baikal in eastern Russia. It was not really an elk, but more closely related to the modern red fallow deer.

We often see Irish elk antlers on walls of big houses or museums because they are so impressive. They could reach 3.6 m (12 ft) across and weigh as much as a 12-year-old child.

Giant Deer

At the end of the Ice Age, the melting glaciers flooded Ireland and created lakes across the entire island. Bodies and antlers from Irish elk that fell into the lakes were preserved in thick mud. Thousands of years later, the lakes had filled with vegetation and become bogs. When local people started digging up the peat for their fires, the preserved bones came to light.

The full skeleton of the Irish elk shows tall spines from the backbone over the shoulders. These would have supported a hump.

Ice Age Venison

Our ancestors hunted the Irish elk for food. From their paintings on cave walls, we know that it was light brown and had a dark stripe along its back. Some paintings show it with a small pointed hump—a fat store—over the shoulders.

We have found bones of Irish elk with marks on them that were made by Stone Age tools.

DID YOU KNOW? The huge antlers were shed every year and had to be grown again for every mating season.

0.2 MYA

Name: *Megaloceros* (Meg–ah–LO–se–ros)
Order: Artiodactyla
Length: 3 m (10 ft)
Weight: 700 kg (1,268 lb)

ANIMAL PROFILE

The antlers were not just for showing off. They were also used as weapons when the males fought one another.

The body of the Irish elk was like that of a modern deer, but much heavier. The forequarters needed much more bulk to support the great antlers.

Glossary

AGE OF MAMMALS
Another term for the Cenozoic period, when mammals began to flourish after the extinction of the dinosaurs.

AMPHIBIAN
An animal that is born in water and breathes underwater using gills when young. As an adult, it usually breathes air using lungs and lives on land or in water.

CALCITE
A common mineral found in limestone.

CAMBRIAN
The first period of the Paleozoic Era, from 541-485 million years ago. Many new forms of life evolved at this time. Scientists have found very few fossils from before the Cambrian.

CARBONIFEROUS
A prehistoric period, 359-299 million years ago, in which there were many swamps and forests on Earth.

CARNIVORE
A meat-eating animal.

CENOZOIC
A prehistoric period from 66 million years ago to the present day. Its beginning was marked by global cooling and the extinction of the dinosaurs, which allowed mammals to flourish and diversify.

CLADE
In biology, a clade is a group of animals that have a common ancestor.

CLASS
In biology, a class is a group of types of animal.

COLD-BLOODED
An animal whose body temperature changes based on the temperature around it. It needs to sunbathe in order to warm up and gain energy.

CONTINENT
A large area of land, sometimes separated from other continents by ocean. Today, there are seven continents: Africa, Antarctica, Asia, Australia, Europe, North America, and South America.

CREST
A growth of bones, scales, feathers, skin, or hair on the head or back of an animal.

CRETACEOUS
A period of Earth's history lasting from 145 to 66 million years ago. During the Cretaceous period, the Earth was warm and wet, with high sea levels. The oceans were full of marine reptiles, while dinosaurs roamed the land. The first flowering plants also evolved during this period. The Cretaceous period began and ended with mass extinction events, when many species died out.

DEVONIAN
A prehistoric period between 410 and 355 million years ago. This time was also known as the Age of Fishes, when the oceans were warm and filled with many new types of fish.

EVOLUTION
The process by which a species changes and adapts over millions of years.

EXTINCTION
When the last living member of an animal species has died.

FAMILY
A group of closely related species.

FERMENTATION
The process of a carbohydrate being chemically broken down by enzymes, usually giving off heat.

FOLIAGE
The leaves of a plant.

FOSSIL
Prehistoric remains, such as bones or footprints, which have become preserved in rock.

FRILL
A bony part of the body that spreads out around the neck of a dinosaur.

GLACIER
A huge body of ice which forms on land and moves slowly downhill.

GRASSLAND
A wide area where most plants are grasses.

HEMISPHERE
Half of the Earth.

HERBIVOROUS
An animal that eats plants.

HIBERNATE
Going to sleep for a long time in winter.

INSECTIVOROUS
An animal that feeds on insects, worms, and other invertebrates.

INSULATION
Any material used to help keep something warm.

INVERTEBRATE
An animal without a backbone.

JURASSIC
A period in Earth's history lasting from 201-145 million years ago. During this warm period, dinosaurs dominated the land. The first birds, lizards, and sharks evolved at this time.

KERATIN
The material that makes up hair, feathers, hoofs, claws, and horns.

MAMMAL
An animal that gives birth to live young and feeds them milk.

METEORITE
A piece of rock or metal that hits the Earth from outer space.

MIGRATE
To move from one area to another, usually at the same time every year.

ORDER
In biology, an order is a group of families of species. Some species also have a super-order, sub-order, or infraorder.

ORDOVICIAN
The Ordovician was a geological period lasting from 485-444 million years ago. The first land plants appeared during this time and many new species of fish evolved.

PARAMAMMAL
A type of animal that probably evolved from reptiles and had some mammal-like features.

PERIOD
In geology, a period is a length of time ranging from millions to tens of millions of years. Each period is based on the rocks recorded from that time.

PERMIAN
A geological period from 299-252 million years ago. At the time, the Earth had one vast desert supercontinent, called Pangea. The period ended with a huge volcanic explosion that killed 80% of marine life and 70% of life on land.

PETRIFIED TREE
A unique type of fossilized wood, where the original wood is slowly replaced by mineral crystals in exactly the same shape.

PLATE
A bony section on the outer body of a dinosaur. Joined together, plates can form a protective covering or stand up from the spine (see *Stegosaurus*, page 64).

PREDATOR
An animal that hunts and eats other animals.

PREY
An animal that is hunted and eaten by other animals.

PRIMATES
An order of mammal that have flexible hands and feet, with either a thumb or a toe set apart from the others, good eyesight, and sometimes a highly developed brain.

QUARRY
An open mine from which rock or other materials are extracted.

REPTILE
An animal that breathes air, usually has scaly skin, and lays eggs on land.

SCAVENGER
A creature that feeds on animals that are already dead.

SILURIAN
The Silurian period lasted from 444-419 million years ago. During that time, many species moved from living in the sea to living on land.

SPECIES
One particular type of living thing. Members of the same species look similar and can produce offspring together.

SQUAMATE GROUP
Squamata is the largest order of reptiles, collectively known as squamates. It includes lizards and snakes.

TENDON
A tough, rope-like tissue in an animal's body, such as the tissue that attaches muscle to bones.

TRIASSIC
A prehistoric period from 252-201 million years ago. Many new species evolved during this period.

TUNDRA
A region which is treeless, cold, windy, and dry. These regions are located in the Arctic and on mountaintops.

VERTEBRA
A small bone that is part of the spine. Many vertebra together make up the backbone in vertebrate animals.

VERTEBRATE
A creature with a backbone, such as birds, mammals, and reptiles.

WARM-BLOODED
An animal that can control its own body temperature. Warm-blooded animals get all their energy supply from food.

Index